Creative and Practical Recipes

Special
Cakes

Publisher's Note: Raw or semi-cooked eggs should not be consumed by babies, toddlers, pregnant or breastfeeding women, the elderly or those suffering from a chronic illness.

Publisher & Creative Director: Nick Wells
Senior Project Editor: Catherine Taylor
Art Director: Mike Spender
Layout Design: Jane Ashley
Digital Design & Production: Chris Herbert

Special thanks to Ann Nicol, Monique Jensen and Frances Bodiam.

For cake decorating supplies, colours and shimmers by mail order: **Squires Kitchen**, Squires Group, Squires House, 3 Waverley Lane, Farnham, Surrey, GU9 8BB. Tel: 0845 617 1801 www.squires-shop.com

Discover 1000s more inspiring baking and decorating ideas, at **lakeland.co.uk**. For embossing tools, moulds, sugarcraft supplies and bakeware by mail order: **Lakeland**, Alexandria Buildings, Windermere, Cumbria, LA23 1BQ. Tel: 01539 488 100.

This is a **FLAME TREE** Book

FLAME TREE PUBLISHING
Crabtree Hall, Crabtree Lane
Fulham, London SW6 6TY
United Kingdom
www.flametreepublishing.com

First published 2014

All pictures © **Flame Tree Publishing Ltd** except the following, which are courtesy **Shutterstock.com** and the following photographers: 4 & 46 & 138, 40b, 70, 94, 162 Ruth Black; 14t Sean van Tonder; 15t M. Unal Ozmen; 16, 21t Sea Wave; 17t Aleksandrs Samuilovs; 17b Ildi Papp; 18t Darkkong; 19t Tharakorn Arunothai; 30 ffolas; 38t donatas1205; 39b Valentin Kolesnicov; 40t Rose-Marie Henriksson; 43t fototip; 43b Giordano Aita; 44, 110 Gyorgy Barna; 46t Agnes Kantaruk; 48b Steve Buckley; 49, 104, 106 Karen H. Ilagan; 50t tratong; 51 Danny E Hooks; 56 Vania Georgieva; 60, 96, 170 Olga Lyubkina; 66 zstock; 72 andras_csontos; 88 Jack Z Young; 100 JFunk; 102 Ksju; 108 Andre Blais; 112 Mariya Volik; 116 BestPhotoStudio; 118 Gordana Sermek; 122 John Kroetch; 130 Elena Schweitzer; 134 Yeko Photo Studio; 146, 156 Elisabeth Coelfen; 184 Dave Clark Digital Photo; 190 Hannamariah; 220 Szasz-Fabian Jozsef. Courtesy **iStockphoto.com** and the following: 114 dwservingHim; 124 GrenouilleFilms.

Creative and Practical Recipes

Special
Cakes

**FLAME TREE
PUBLISHING**

Contents

Essentials

It's no use trying to create or decorate a cake when you know nothing about the tools and techniques needed to do so. Luckily, this section provides you with all of that information! From all the essential equipment such as tins and icing bags, to key baking ingredients, methods and basic recipes for fruit cake, chocolate cake, madeira cake, cupcakes, icings and how to use them, you'll be prepared for any recipe you choose (or indeed, you could come up with your own!).

Equipment  Utensils

Nowadays, you can get lost in the cookware sections of some of the larger stores – they really are a cook's paradise, with gadgets, cooking tools and state-of-the-art electronic blenders, mixers and liquidisers. A few well-picked, high-quality utensils and pieces of equipment will be frequently used and will therefore be a much wiser buy than cheaper gadgets.

Cooking equipment not only assists in the kitchen, but can make all the difference between success and failure. Take the humble cake tin: although a very basic piece of cooking equipment, it plays an essential role in baking. Using the incorrect size, for example, a tin that is too large, will spread the mixture too thinly and the result will be a flat, limp-looking cake. On the other hand, cramming the mixture into a tin which is too small will result in the mixture rising up and out of the tin.

Bakeware

To ensure successful baking, it is worth investing in a selection of high-quality tins, which, if looked after properly, should last for many years. Follow the manufacturers' instructions when first using and ensure that the tins are thoroughly washed and dried after use and before putting away.

~ Sandwich Cake Tins – Perhaps the most useful of tins are sandwich cake tins, ideal for classics such as Victoria Sponge or a Whisked Sponge Cake. You will need two tins and they are normally 18 cm/7 inches or 20.5 cm/8 inches in diameter and are about 5–7.5 cm/ 2–3 inches deep. They are often nonstick.

∾ Deep Cake Tins – With deep cake tins, it is personal choice whether you buy round or square tins and they vary in size from 12.5–35.5 cm/ 5–14 inches with a depth of between 12.5–15 cm/5–6 inches. A deep cake tin for everyday fruit or Madeira cake is a must – a useful size is 20.5 cm/8 inches.

∾ Loaf Tins – Loaf tins are used for fruit or tea breads, and normally come in two sizes, 450 g/1 lb and 900 g/2 lb.

∾ Muffin and Bun Trays – Muffin trays – for muffins and cupcakes – come in different weights and sizes; they are generally available with six or 12 deep-set holes. When purchasing metal trays, buy the heaviest type you can – these produce the best results, as they have good heat distribution and do not buckle. If not using nonstick trays it is advisable to grease before use with margarine or butter. You will normally need to line metal trays with paper cases or strips of baking parchment. You can also buy reusable silicone muffin trays, which are flexible and produce very good results.

∾ Cupcake Cases – Paper and reusable silicone cupcake cases come in many colours and patterns and several sizes, from mini to medium/standard to deep/large. It is worth buying the more expensive ones, which are thicker, resulting in a better shape and less penetration of oil and moisture.

∾ Cake Pop Baking Moulds – These are silicone or metal tins that come in two halves and have 12 small round indentations for the cake mix. Fill one half of the tin and clamp the other tin on top and, as the mixture rises, it will form perfect spheres. The round cakes are placed on thin lollipop sticks before decorating.

∾ Other Tins – Square or oblong shallow baking tins are also very useful for making tray bakes, fudge brownies, flapjacks and shortbread. Swiss roll tins are even shallower, like a baking tray but with sides all around. Then there are patty tins; ideal for making small buns; and individual Yorkshire pudding tins or flan tins. They are available in a variety of sizes.

There are plenty of other tins to choose from, ranging from themed tins, such as Christmas trees, numbers and petals, to ring mould tins (tins with a hole in the centre) and spring-form tins, where the sides release after cooking, allowing the finished cake to be removed easily. A selection of roasting tins are also a worthwhile investment, as they can double up as a bain marie, or for cooking larger quantities of cakes such as gingerbread.

Other Essential Equipment

∾ Measuring Spoons, Scales and Jugs – Baking needs 100 per cent accuracy to achieve a perfect result. A set of standard measuring spoons for accurate measuring of small quantities of ingredients is vital. Remember that all spoon measures should be level and do not use cutlery such as kitchen tablespoons or teaspoons, as these sizes differ and may be inaccurate.

Measuring jugs are also necessary for any larger amounts of liquids, and scales for solids. Scales come in many shapes and sizes, both digital and with weights. Most have a weigh pan, although with some your own bowl is used.

Sieves – Use a large, wire sieve for sifting flour and dry ingredients together and keep a smaller one, ideally nylon, aside just for icing sugars.

Mixing Bowls – You will need a set of different-size mixing bowls for beating small and large amounts of mixture, frostings and icings. They are also useful for melting ingredients (for which they need to be glass).

Wooden Spoon – Keep an old-fashioned, large wooden spoon aside for baking, for beating butters and creaming. Do not use one that has been used for frying savoury things such as onions, as the flavours will taint the cake mixture.

Kitchen Scissors – Scissors are essential for many small jobs, including cutting papers to size and snipping cherries, dried fruits or nuts into chunks.

Grater – A grater is useful for grating citrus zests, chocolate and marzipan. Choose one with a fine and a coarse side.

Spatula – An angled spatula, usually plastic or silicone, is useful for scraping and transferring mixture from the mixing bowl to the tin and spreading the mixture once it is in the tin.

Pastry Brush – A pastry brush is used for brushing glazes over cakes and melted butter round trays. As brushes tend to wear out regularly and shed their bristles, keep a spare new brush to hand.

Equipment & Utensils

∽ Cake Tester or Skewer – Use a small, thin, metal skewer for inserting into the centre of a cake to test if it is ready. This is a handy piece of equipment but, if you do not have one, a clean, thin, metal knitting needle may be used instead.

∽ Palette Knife – A long, metal spatula is useful for easing cakes out of their tins once cooked.

∽ Wire Cooling Racks – Racks are vital to allow air to circulate round the hot cakes to let them cool down quickly, which prevents them from becoming moist or soggy underneath. A wire rack also protects your kitchen surfaces from the heat.

∽ Piping Bags and Nozzles – A nylon piping bag that comes with a set of five nozzles is a very useful piece of equipment for decorating with icings. Look for a set with a plain nozzle and various star nozzles for piping swirls round cupcakes. The larger the star nozzle, the wider the swirls will be on the finished cakes. Disposable paper or clear plastic icing bags are available, but nylon piping bags can be washed out in warm soapy water and dried out, ready to reuse again and again.

∽ To Make a Paper Icing Bag – Cut out a 38 x 25.5 cm/15 x 10 inch rectangle of greaseproof paper. Fold it diagonally in half to form two triangular shapes. Cut along the fold line to make two triangles. One of these triangles can be used another time – it is quicker and easier to make two at a time from one square than to measure and mark out a triangle on a sheet of paper.

Fold one of the points on the long side of the triangle over the top to make a sharp cone and hold in the centre. Fold the other sharp end of the triangle over the cone. Hold all the points together at the back of the cone, keeping the pointed end sharp. Turn the points inside the top edge, fold over to make a crease, then secure with a piece of sticky tape.

To use, snip away the end, place a piping nozzle in position and fill the bag with icing, or fill the bag with icing first, then snip away a tiny hole at the end for piping a plain edge, writing or piping tiny dots.Basic mixing cutlery is also essential, such as a wooden spoon (for mixing and creaming), a spatula (for transferring the mixture from the mixing bowl to the baking tins and spreading the mixture once it is in the tins) and a palette knife (to ease cakes and breads out of their tins before placing them on the wire racks to cool). Measuring spoons are essential for accurate measuring of both dry and wet ingredients.

Electrical Equipment

Nowadays, help from time-saving gadgets and electrical equipment make baking far easier and quicker. Equipment can be used for creaming, mixing, beating, whisking, kneading, grating and chopping. There is a wide choice of machines available, from the most basic to the very sophisticated.

Equipment & Utensils

❧ Food Processors – First, decide what you need your processor to do when choosing a machine. If you are a novice to baking, it may be a waste to start with a machine which offers a wide range of implements and functions. This can be off-putting and result in not using the machine to its ultimate potential.

In general, while styling and product design play a role in the price, the more you pay, the larger the machine will be, with a bigger bowl capacity and many more gadgets attached. However, just what basic features should you ensure your machine has before buying it?

When buying a food processor, look for measurements on the side of the processor bowl and machines with a removable feed tube which allows food or liquid to be added while the motor is running. Look out for machines that have the facility to increase the capacity of the bowl and have a pulse button for controlled chopping.

For many people, storage is an issue, so reversible discs and flex storage, or, on more advanced models, a blade storage compartment or box, can be a real advantage.

It is also worth thinking about machines which offer optional extras, which can be bought as your cooking requirements change. Mini-chopping bowls are available for those wanting to chop small quantities of food. If time is an issue, dishwasher-friendly attachments may be vital. Citrus presses, liquidisers and whisks may all be useful attachments for the individual cook.

Blenders – Blenders often come as attachments to food processors and are generally used for liquidising and puréeing foods. There are two main types of blender. The first is known as a goblet blender. The blades of this blender are at the bottom of the goblet, with measurements up the sides.

The second blender is portable. It is hand-held and should be placed in a bowl to blend.

Food Mixers – These are ideally suited to mixing cakes, either as a table-top mixer or a hand-held mixer. Both are extremely useful and based on the same principle of mixing or whisking in an open bowl to allow more air to get to the mixture and therefore give a lighter texture.

The table-top mixers are freestanding and are capable of dealing with fairly large quantities of mixture. They are robust machines, capable of dealing easily with kneading dough and heavy cake mixing, as well as whipping cream, whisking egg whites or making one-stage cakes. These mixers also offer a wide range of attachments ranging from liquidisers, mincers, juicers, can openers and many more and varied attachments.

Hand-held mixers are smaller than freestanding ones and often come with their own bowl and stand, from which they can be lifted off and used as hand-held devices. They have a motorised head with detachable twin whisks. These mixers are particularly versatile, as they do not need a specific bowl in which to whisk. Any suitable mixing bowl can be used.

Essential Baking Ingredients

The quantities may differ, but basic baking ingredients do not vary greatly. Let us take a closer look at the baking ingredients which are essential.

Fat

Butter and firm block margarine are the fats most commonly used in baking. Others can also be used, such as white vegetable fat, lard and oil. Low-fat spreads are not recommended, as they tend to break down when they are cooked at a very high temperature. Often, it is simply a matter of personal preference which fat you decide to use when baking, but there are still a few guidelines that it is very important to remember.

Unsalted butter is the fat most commonly used in cake making, especially in rich fruit cakes and the heavier sponge cakes such as Madeira or chocolate torte. Unsalted butter gives a distinctive flavour to the cake. Some people favour margarine, which imparts little or no flavour to the cake.

As a rule, firm margarine and butter should not be used straight from the refrigerator but allowed to come to room temperature before using. Also, it should be beaten by itself first before creaming or rubbing in. Soft margarine is best suited to one-stage recipes.

If oil is used, care should be taken – it is a good idea to follow a specific recipe, as the proportions of oil to flour and eggs are different.

Fat is an integral ingredient when making pastry; again, there are a few specific guidelines to bear in mind. For shortcrust pastry, the best results are achieved by using equal amounts of lard or white vegetable fat with butter or block margarine. The amount of fat used is always half the amount of flour. Other pastries use differing amounts of ingredients. Pâte sucrée (a sweet flan pastry) uses all butter with eggs and a little sugar, while flaky or puff pastry uses a larger proportion of fat to flour and relies on the folding and rolling during making to ensure that the pastry rises and flakes well. When using a recipe, refer to the instructions to obtain the best result.

Flour

We can buy a wide range of flour, all designed for specific jobs. Strong flour, which is rich in gluten, whether it is white or brown (this includes granary and stoneground), is best kept for bread and Yorkshire pudding. It is also recommended for steamed suet puddings, as well as puff pastry. '00' flour is designed for pasta making and there is no substitute for this flour.

Essential Baking Ingredients

Ordinary flour or weak flour is best for cakes, biscuits and sauces, which absorb the fat easily and give a soft, light texture. This flour comes in plain white or self-raising, as well as wholemeal.

Self-raising flour, which has the raising agent already incorporated, is best kept for sponge cakes, where it is important that an even rise is achieved. Plain flour can be used for all types of baking and sauces. If using plain flour for scones or cakes and puddings, unless otherwise stated in the recipe, use 1 teaspoon of baking powder to 225 g/8 oz of plain flour.

With sponge cakes and light fruit cakes, it is best to use self-raising flour, as the raising agent has already been added to the flour. This way, there is no danger of using too much, which can result in a sunken cake with a sour taste.

There are other raising agents that are also used. Some cakes use bicarbonate of soda with or without cream of tartar, blended with warm or sour milk. Whisked eggs also act as a raising agent, as the air trapped in the egg ensures that the mixture rises. Generally, no other raising agent is required.

Some flour also comes ready-sifted which can be a benefit when using it for baking. There is even a special sponge flour designed especially for whisked sponges. Also, it is possible to buy flours that cater for coeliacs, which contain no gluten. Buckwheat, soya and chickpea flours are also available.

Eggs

When a recipe states '1 egg', it is generally accepted that this refers to a medium egg. Over the past few years, the grading of eggs has changed. For years, eggs were sold as small, standard and large, then this method changed and they were graded in numbers, with 1 being the largest. The general feeling by the public was that this system was misleading, so now we buy our eggs as small, medium and large.

Due to the slight risk of salmonella, all eggs are now sold date-stamped to ensure that the eggs are used in their prime. This applies even to farm eggs, which are no longer allowed to be sold straight from the farm. Look for the lion quality stamp (on 75 percent of all eggs sold), which guarantees that the eggs come from hens vaccinated against salmonella, have been laid in the UK and are produced to the highest food safety and standards. All of these eggs carry a best-before date.

There are many types of eggs sold and it really is a question of personal preference which ones are chosen. All offer the same nutritional benefits. The majority of eggs sold in this country are from caged hens. These are the cheapest eggs and the hens have been fed on a manufactured mixed diet. Eggs should be stored in their box in the refrigerator, and kept away from foods with strong smells.

Essential Baking Ingredients

Barn eggs are from hens kept in barns who are free to roam within the barn. However, their diet is similar to caged hens and the barns may be overcrowded.

It is commonly thought that free-range eggs are from hens that lead a much more natural life and are fed natural foods. This, however, is not always the case and in some instances, they may still live in a crowded environment.

Four-grain eggs are from hens that have been fed on grain and no preventative medicines have been included in their diet. Organic eggs are from hens that live in a flock, whose beaks are not clipped and who are completely free to roam. Obviously, these eggs are much more expensive than the others.

Store eggs in the refrigerator with the round end uppermost (as packed in the egg boxes). Allow to come to room temperature before using. Do remember, raw or semi-cooked eggs should not be given to babies, toddlers, pregnant women, the elderly or those suffering from a recurring illness.

Sugar

Sugar not only offers taste to baking, but also adds texture and volume to the mixture. It is generally accepted that caster sugar is best for sponge cakes, puddings and meringues. Its fine granules disperse evenly when creaming or whisking. Granulated sugar is used for more general cooking, such as stewing fruit, whereas demerara sugar, with its toffee taste and crunchy texture, is good for sticky puddings and cakes such as flapjacks. For rich fruit cakes as well as Christmas puddings and cakes, use the muscovado sugars, which give a rich, intense molasses or treacle flavour.

Icing sugar is fine and powdery and is used primarily for icings. If used for icings it can be coloured using a few drops of food colouring or flavoured using citrus juice, cocoa powder or coffee extract. Icing sugar can also be used in meringues and in fruit sauces when the sugar needs to dissolve quickly. Always sift icing sugar at least once before use to remove lumps which would prevent a smooth texture from being achieved.

For a different taste, try flavouring your own sugar. Place a vanilla pod in a screw-top jar, fill with caster sugar, screw down the lid and leave for 2–3 weeks before using. Top up after use. Use thinly pared lemon or orange rind in the same manner.

If trying to reduce sugar intake, then use the unrefined varieties, such as golden granulated, golden caster, unrefined demerara and the muscovado sugars. All of these are a little sweeter than their refined counterparts, so less is required. Alternatively, clear honey or fructose (fruit sugar) can reduce sugar intake, as they have similar calories to sugar, but are twice as sweet. Also, they have a slow release, so their effect lasts longer. Dried fruits can also be included in the diet to top up sugar intake.

🐾   Essential Baking Ingredients

Basic Methods

Lining

If a recipe states that the tin needs lining, do not be tempted to ignore this. Rich fruit cakes and other cakes that take a long time to cook benefit from the tin being lined so that the edges and base do not burn or dry out.

∾ Papers – Greaseproof paper or nonstick baking parchment is ideal for this. It is a good idea to have the paper at least double thickness, or preferably three to four layers. Sponge cakes and other cakes that are cooked in 30 minutes or less are also better if the bases are lined, as it is far easier to remove them from the tin.

∾ Technique – The best way to line a round or square tin is to draw lightly around the base and then cut just inside the markings, making it easy to sit in the tin. Next, lightly oil the paper so it peels away easily from the cake. If the sides of the tin also need to be lined, then cut a strip of paper slightly longer than the circumference of the tin (this can be measured by wrapping a piece of string around the rim of the tin) and a few inches higher. Fold it back about an inch along its length, then snip angled cuts at intervals up to the fold. Once again, lightly oil the paper, push against the tin and oil once more, as this will hold the paper to the sides.

Separating Eggs

When separating eggs (that is, separating the white from the yolk), crack an egg in half lightly and cleanly over a bowl, being careful not to break the yolk and keeping it in the shell. Then tip the yolk backwards and forwards between the two shell halves, allowing as much of the white as possible to spill out into the bowl. Keep or discard the yolk and/or the white as needed. Make sure that you do not get any yolk in your whites, as this will prevent successful whisking of the whites. It takes practice!

Different Mixing Technique

∾ Creaming – Light cakes are made by the creaming method, which means that the butter and sugar are first beaten or 'creamed' together. A little care is needed for this method. Using a large mixing bowl, beat the fat and sugar together until pale and fluffy. The eggs are gradually beaten in to form a slackened batter and the flour is folded in last, to stiffen up the mixture. In some recipes, egg whites are whisked and added to the mixture separately for extra lightness.

When the eggs are added, they are best used at room temperature to prevent the mixture from splitting or 'curdling'. Adding a teaspoon of flour with each beaten egg will help to keep the mixture light and smooth and prevent the mixture from separating. A badly mixed,

curdled batter will hold less air and be heavy or can cause a sunken cake.

Fruit cakes are also usually made by the creaming method, then dried fruit and nuts are folded into the mixture last.

∾ Rubbing In – In this method, the fat is lightly worked into the flour between the fingers, as in pastry-making, until the mixture resembles fine crumbs. This can be done by hand or in a food processor. Enough liquid is stirred in to give a soft mixture that will drop easily from a spoon. This method is used for easy fruit cakes.

∾ All-In-One Mixtures – This 'one-stage' method is quick and easy and is perfect for those new to baking, as it does not involve any complicated techniques. It is ideal for making light sponges, but soft tub-type margarine or softened butter at room temperature must be used. All the ingredients are simply placed in a large bowl and quickly beaten together for just a few minutes until smooth. Be careful not to overbeat, as this will make the mixture too wet. Self-raising flour with the addition of a little extra baking powder is vital for a good rise.

∾ The Melting Method – Cakes with a delicious moist sticky texture, such as gingerbread, are made by this method. These cakes use a high proportion of sugar and syrup, which are gently warmed together in a saucepan with the fat, until the sugar has dissolved and the mixture is liquid. It is important to cool the hot melted mixture a little before beating in flour, eggs and spices to make the batter, otherwise it will damage the power of the raising agent.

Basic Recipes

~c~

Rich Fruit Cake

Square Cake Size	13 cm/5 inch square	16 cm/6 inch square	18 cm/7 inch square
Round Cake Size	15 cm/6 inch round	18 cm/7 inch round	20 cm/8 inch round
sultanas	125 g/4 oz	175 g/6 oz	225 g/8 oz
raisins	125 g/4 oz	175 g/6 oz	225 g/8 oz
currants	125 g/4 oz	175 g/6 oz	225 g/8 oz
chopped mixed peel	50 g/2 oz	75 g/3 oz	125 g/4 oz
glacé cherries, chopped	50 g/2 oz	75 g/3 oz	125 g/4 oz
lemons	$1/2$	$1/2$	1
dark rum or fresh orange juice	2 tbsp	3 tbsp	4 tbsp
butter, softened	125 g/4 oz	175 g/6 oz	225 g/8 oz
soft dark muscovado sugar	125 g/4 oz	175 g/6 oz	225 g/8 oz
plain flour	125 g/4 oz	175 g/6 oz	225 g/8 oz
mixed spice	$1/2$ tsp	1 tsp	2 tsp
ground almonds	25 g/1 oz	50 g/2 oz	75 g/3 oz
eggs, beaten	2	3	4–5
dark treacle	2 tsp	1 tbsp	1 tbsp
Cooking time 1	30 mins	50 mins	1 hour
Cooking time 2	1 hour 30 mins	1 hour 40 mins	$2^{1}/_{4}$ hours

Rich Fruit Cake cont'd

Square Cake Size	20 cm/8 inch square	23 cm/9 inch square	25 cm/10 inch square
Round Cake Size	23 cm/9 inch round	25 cm/10 inch round	28 cm/11 inch round
sultanas	275 g/10 oz	350 g/12 oz	450 g/1 lb
raisins	275 g/10 oz	350 g/12 oz	450 g/1 lb
currants	275 g/10 oz	350 g/12 oz	450 g/1 lb
chopped mixed peel	150 g/5 oz	175 g/6 oz	200 g/7 oz
glace cherries, chopped	150 g/5 oz	175 g/6 oz	200 g/7 oz
lemons	1	$1^1/_2$	2
dark rum or fresh orange juice	2 tbsp	4 tbsp	6 tbsp
butter, softened	275 g/10 oz	350 g/12 oz	450 g/1 lb
soft dark muscovado sugar	275 g/10 oz	350 g/12 oz	450 g/1 lb
plain flour	275 g/10 oz	350 g/12 oz	450 g/1 lb
mixed spice	15 ml/1 tbsp	15 ml/1 tbsp	15 ml/1 tbsp
ground almonds	125 g/4 oz	125 g/4 oz	150 g/5 oz
eggs, beaten	5–6	6	8
dark treacle	1 tbsp	1 tbsp	2 tbsp
Cooking time 1	1 hour 30 mins	1 hour 50 mins	2 hours
Cooking time 2	$2^1/_2$–3 hours	3 hours	$3^1/_4$ hours

Before you start to bake, place the sultanas, raisins, currants, peel and cherries in a large bowl. Finely grate in the zest from the lemon and add the dark rum or freshly squeezed orange juice. Stir, cover and leave to soak overnight, or for 24 hours if possible.

Preheat the oven to 150˚C/300˚F/Gas Mark 2. Grease and line the tin with a triple layer of nonstick baking parchment.

Cream the butter and muscovado sugar in a large bowl until light and fluffy. Sift the flour and mixed spice together in a separate bowl, then stir in the ground almonds.

Add the eggs to the creamed mixture, a little at a time, adding a teaspoon of flour with each addition. Fold the remaining flour into the bowl, then add the treacle and soaked fruits. Stir well until the mixture is soft, smooth and well blended.

Spoon the mixture into the tin, then make a hollow in the centre of the mixture with the back of a large spoon, to stop it peaking too much in the middle.

Tie a layer of newspaper round the outside of the tin and bake according to cooking time 1, then reduce the heat to 120°C/250°F/ Gas Mark 1/2 for cooking time 2.

If the top of the cake starts to brown too much, cover with a layer of damp, crumpled baking parchment. Test the cake by inserting a skewer into the centre; it should come out with no mixture sticking to it.

Cool the cake in the tin and then remove, leaving the lining papers on. Wrap the cake in an extra layer of baking parchment, then tightly in foil and leave to mature for 1–3 months in a cool place.

Basic Recipes

Rich Chocolate Cake

Square Cake Size	13 cm/5 inch square	18 cm/7 inch square	23 cm/9 inch square
Round Cake Size	15 cm/6 inch round	20 cm/8 inch round	25 cm/10 inch round
plain chocolate	50 g/2 oz	125 g/4 oz	225 g/8 oz
soft dark brown sugar	150 g/5 oz	275 g/10 oz	575g/1^1/$_4$lb 3oz
milk	135 ml/4^1/$_2$ fl oz	200 ml/7 fl oz	500 ml/18 fl oz
butter, softened	50 g/2 oz	125 g/4 oz	225 g/8 oz
eggs, beaten	1	3	6
plain flour	125 g/4 oz	225 g/8 oz	450 g/1 lb
bicarbonate of soda	^{1}/$_2$ tsp	1 tsp	2 tsp
Cooking time	45 mins	1 hour	1^1/$_2$ hours

Preheat the oven to 180˚C/350˚F/Gas Mark 4. Grease and line the tin with nonstick baking parchment. Break the chocolate into small pieces and place in a heavy-based pan with one third of the sugar and all of the milk. Heat gently until the chocolate has melted, then remove from the heat and cool.

Beat the butter and remaining sugar together until fluffy, then beat in the eggs a little at a time. Gradually beat in the cold melted chocolate mixture.

Sift the flour and bicarbonate of soda into the mixture and fold together with a large metal spoon until smooth. Bake for the time shown on the chart or until a skewer inserted into the centre comes out clean.

Cool for 10 minutes, then turn out of the tin onto a wire rack to cool. Store wrapped in foil until needed, or freeze wrapped tightly in foil for up to 3 months.

Madeira Cake

Square Cake Size	13 cm/5 inch square	16 cm/6 inch square	18 cm/7 inch square
Round Cake Size	15 cm/6 inch round	18 cm/7 inch round	20 cm/8 inch round
butter, softened	175 g/6 oz	225 g/8 oz	350 g/12 oz
caster sugar	175 g/6 oz	225 g/8 oz	350 g/12 oz
self-raising flour	175 g/6 oz	225 g/8 oz	350 g/12 oz
plain flour	75 g/3 oz	125 g/4 oz	175 g/6 oz
eggs	3	4	6
vanilla extract	$1/2$ tsp	1 tsp	1 tsp
glycerine	1 tsp	1 tsp	1 tsp
Cooking time	1 hour	1–$1^1/4$ hours	$1^1/4$–$1^1/2$ hours

Square Cake Size	20 cm/8 inch square	23 cm/9 inch square
Round Cake Size	23 cm/9 inch round	25 cm/10 inch round
butter, softened	450 g/1 lb	500 g/1 lb 2 oz
caster sugar	450 g/1 lb	500 g/1 lb 2 oz
self-raising flour	450 g/1 lb	500 g/1 lb 2 oz
plain flour	225 g/8 oz	250 g/9 oz
eggs	8	9
vanilla extract	2 tsp	1 tbsp
glycerine	2 tsp	1 tbsp
Cooking time	$1^1/2$ – $1^3/4$ hours	$1^1/2$ – $1^3/4$ hours

  Basic Recipes

Preheat the oven to 160°C/325°F/Gas Mark 3. Grease and line the tin with nonstick baking parchment.

Cream the butter and caster sugar together in a large bowl until light and fluffy. Sift the flours together. Whisk the eggs into the mixture one at a time, adding a teaspoon of flour with each addition to prevent the mixture from curdling.

Add the remaining flour, the vanilla extract and glycerine to the mixture and fold together with a large metal spoon until the mixture is smooth.

Spoon into the tin and bake for the time shown on the chart until firm and well risen and a skewer inserted into the centre comes out clean.

Leave to cool in the tin for 10 minutes, then turn out onto a wire rack to cool. Wrap in foil and store for up to 3 days before decorating. Freeze wrapped in foil for up to 2 months.

∽ Bowl Shaped – To cook the cake in a 2 litre/4 pint ovenproof bowl, grease the bowl well and use the amounts for the 13 cm/5 inch square cake, baking for 45 minutes–1 hour.

∽ Lemon Variation – To make the lemon variation of the Madeira cake, you can simply omit the vanilla extract and add the same amount of finely grated lemon zest.

∽ Almond Variation – To make the almond variation of the Madeira cake, you can simply omit the vanilla extract and add the same amount of almond extract.

Basic Vanilla Cupcakes

Makes 12–14

125 g/4 oz caster sugar
125 g/4 oz soft tub margarine
2 medium eggs
125 g/4 oz self-raising flour
½ tsp baking powder
½ tsp vanilla extract

Preheat the oven to 190°C/375°F/Gas Mark 5.
Line a bun tray with paper cases.

Place all the cupcake ingredients in a large bowl
and beat with an electric mixer for about 2 minutes
until light and smooth. Fill the paper cases halfway
up with the mixture. Bake for about 15 minutes
until firm, risen and golden.

Remove to a wire rack to cool. Keeps for 2–3 days in an airtight container. Can be frozen
for up to 2 months, but the paper cases will come away when thawed and these will
need replacing.

∾ Chocolate Variation – Omit the caster sugar and use soft light brown sugar
   instead. Sift 25 g/1 oz cocoa powder in with the flour and baking powder. Omit the
   vanilla extract and add 2 tbsp milk instead. Mix and bake as above.

∾ Cherry & Almond Variation – Add 50 g/2 oz finely chopped washed
   glacé cherries. Omit the vanilla extract and use almond extract instead.
   Mix and bake as above.

All-in-one Quick-mix Sponge

To make sure you end up with the correct quantity of mixture for your tin when making an all-in-one sponge mix, use the guidelines below to select the ingredient quantities depending on tin size and shape.

Tin size and shape	Two 18 cm/7 inch sandwich tins	Two 20 cm/8 inch sandwich tins
Caster sugar	125 g/4 oz	175 g/6 oz
Soft tub margarine	125 g/4 oz	175 g/6 oz
Eggs	2	3
Self-raising flour	125 g/4 oz	175 g/6 oz
Baking powder	1 tsp	1 tsp
Vanilla extract	½ tsp	1 tsp
Baking time	25–30 mins	30–35 mins

Tin size and shape	13 cm/5 inch square	16 cm/6 inch square
Tin size and shape	15 cm/6 inch round	18 cm/7 inch round
Caster sugar	125 g/4 oz	175 g/6 oz
Soft tub margarine	125 g/4 oz	175 g/6 oz
Eggs	2	3
Self-raising flour	125 g/4 oz	175 g/6 oz
Baking powder	1 tsp	1 tsp
Vanilla extract	½ tsp	1 tsp
Baking time	30–35 mins	35–40 mins

Tin size and shape	18 cm/7 inch square	20 cm/8 inch square
Tin size and shape	20 cm/8 inch round	23 cm/9 inch round
Caster sugar	225 g/8 oz	350 g/12 oz
Soft tub margarine	225 g/8 oz	350 g/12 oz
Eggs	4	6
Self-raising flour	225 g/8 oz	350 g/12 oz
Baking powder	1½ tsp	2 tsp
Vanilla extract	1 tsp	2 tsp
Baking time	45–55 mins	50–60 mins

Tin size and shape	28 x 18 x 4 cm/11 x 7 x 1½ inch slab cake	30 x 25 x 5 cm/12 x 10 x 2 inch slab cake
Caster sugar	175 g/6 oz	275 g/10 oz
Soft tub margarine	175 g/6 oz	275 g/10 oz
Eggs	3	5
Self-raising flour	175 g/6 oz	275 g/10 oz
Baking powder	1 tsp	2 tsp
Vanilla extract	1 tsp	2 tsp
Baking time	30–40 mins	50–60 mins

Preheat the oven to 160°C/325°F/Gas Mark 3. Grease and line the tin with nonstick baking parchment, or butter the pudding basins well.

Place the sugar, margarine and eggs in a large mixing bowl. Sift in the flour and baking powder and add the vanilla extract. (Continued overleaf.)

🍃   Basic Recipes

Pudding basin size	900 ml/1½ pint	1.1 litre/2 pint
Caster sugar	125 g/4 oz	175 g/6 oz
Soft tub margarine	125 g/4 oz	175 g/6 oz
Eggs	2	3
Self-raising flour	125 g/ 4 oz	175 g/6 oz
Baking powder	1 tsp	1 tsp
Vanilla extract	½ tsp	1 tsp
Baking time	50 mins	1 hour

Beat the ingredients together with an electric mixer for 1–2 minutes until they are smooth and well combined. Spoon into the tins or basin and bake according to the time guideline above or until the cake appears well risen, just firm to the touch and is beginning to shrink away from the sides of the tin or basin.

Cool in the tin for 4 minutes, then turn out onto a wire rack to cool. Peel away the papers while still warm.

For variations:

∾ Chocolate Variation – Omit the vanilla extract and add 1 tbsp softened cocoa powder for the 2-egg mix, 1½ tbsp for the 3-egg mix, 2 tbsp for the 4-egg mix and 3 tbsp for the 5-egg mix.

∾ Orange or Lemon Variation – Omit the vanilla extract and add 2 tsp finely grated orange or lemon zest for the 2-egg mix, 3 tsp for the 3-egg mix, 4 tsp for the 4-egg mix and 2 tbsp for the 5-egg mix.

∾ Coffee Variation – Omit the vanilla extract and add 1 tbsp coffee essence for the 2-egg mix, 1½ tbsp for the 3-egg mix, 2 tbsp for the 4-egg mix and 2½ tbsp for the 5-egg mix.

Handling Chocolate & Caramel

C

Tips & Techniques

There are a few useful techniques for working with chocolate. None of them is very complicated, and all can be mastered easily with a little practice. These general guidelines apply equally for all types of chocolate,

Melting Chocolate

All types of chocolate are sensitive to temperature, so care needs to be taken during the melting process. It is also worth noting that different brands of chocolate have different consistencies when melting and when melted. Experiment with different brands to find one that you like.

As a general rule, it is important not to allow any water to come into contact with the chocolate. In fact, a drop or two of water is more dangerous than larger amounts, which may blend in. The melted chocolate will seize and it will be impossible to bring it back to a smooth consistency.

Do not overheat chocolate or melt it by itself in a pan over a direct heat. Always use either a double boiler or a heatproof bowl set over a saucepan of water, but do not allow the bottom of the bowl to come into contact with the water, as this will overheat the chocolate. Keep an eye on the chocolate, checking it every couple of minutes and reducing or extinguishing the heat under the saucepan as necessary.

🐚 Handling Chocolate

Stir the chocolate once or twice during melting until it is smooth and no lumps remain. Do not cover the bowl once the chocolate has melted or condensation will form, water will drop into it and it will be ruined. If the chocolate turns from a glossy, liquid mass into a dull, coarse, textured mess, you will have to start again.

Microwaving is another way of melting chocolate, but again, caution is required. Follow the oven manufacturer's instructions together with the instructions on the chocolate and proceed with care. Melt the chocolate in bursts of 30–60 seconds, stirring well between bursts, until the chocolate is smooth. If possible, stop microwaving before all the chocolate has melted and allow the residual heat in the chocolate to finish the job. The advantage of microwaving is that you do not need to use a saucepan, making the whole job quicker and neater.

Making Chocolate Decorations

∞ Curls and Caraque – Chocolate curls are made using a clean paint scraper. They are usually large, fully formed curls, which are useful for decorating gateaux and cakes. Caraque are long, thin curls, which can be used in the same way, but are less dramatic.

To make either shape, melt the chocolate following your preferred method and then spread it in a thin layer over a cool surface, such as a marble slab, ceramic tile or piece of granite. Leave until just set but not hard. To make curls, take the clean paint scraper and set it at an angle to the surface of the chocolate, then push, taking a layer off the surface. This will curl until you release the pressure.

To make caraque, use a large, sharp knife and hold it at about a 45-degree angle to the chocolate. Hold the handle and the tip and scrape the knife towards you, pulling the handle but keeping the tip more or less in the same place. This method makes thinner, tighter, longer curls.

● Shaved Chocolate – Using a vegetable peeler, shave a thick block of chocolate to make minicurls. These are best achieved if the chocolate is a little soft, otherwise it has a tendency to break into little flakes.

● Chocolate Shapes – Spread a thin layer of chocolate, as described in the instructions for chocolate curls, and allow to set as before. Use shaped cutters or a sharp knife to cut out shapes. Use to decorate cakes.

● Chocolate Butterflies – Draw a butterfly shape on a piece of nonstick baking parchment. Fold the paper down the middle of the body of the butterfly to make a crease, then open the paper out flat. Pipe chocolate onto the outline of the butterfly, then fill in the wings with loose zigzag lines. Carefully fold the paper so the wings are at right angles, supporting them from underneath in the corner of a large tin or with some other support, and leave until set. Peel away the paper to use.

● Chocolate Leaves – Many types of leaf are suitable, but ensure they are not poisonous before using. Rose leaves are easy to find and make good shapes. Wash and dry the leaves carefully before using. Melt the chocolate, following the instructions given at the beginning of this section. Using a small paintbrush, paint a thin layer of chocolate onto the back of the leaf. Allow to set before adding another thin layer. When set, carefully peel off the leaf. Chocolate leaves are also very attractive when made using two different types of chocolate, white and dark chocolate, for example. Paint half the leaf first with one type of chocolate and allow to set before painting the other half with the second chocolate. Leave to set, then peel off the leaf.

Handling Chocolate

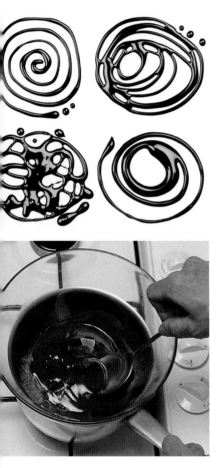

~ Chocolate Lace – Make a nonstick baking parchment piping bag. Draw an outline of the required shape onto nonstick baking parchment, a triangle, for example. Pipe chocolate evenly onto the outline, fill in the centre with lacy squiggles and leave until set. Remove the paper to use.

~ Chocolate Squiggles – Use a teaspoon of melted chocolate to drizzle random shapes onto nonstick baking parchment. Leave to set and remove paper to use. Alternatively, pipe a zigzag line about 5 cm/2 inches long onto a piece of nonstick baking parchment. Pipe a straight line, slightly longer at either end, down the middle of the zigzag.

~ Chocolate Modelling Paste – Chocolate modelling paste is very useful for cake coverings, as well as for making heavier shapes to decorate your cakes, such as ribbons. To make the paste, simply follow these instructions:

Put 200 g/7 oz dark chocolate in a bowl and add 3 tablespoons of liquid glucose. Set the bowl over a pan of gently simmering water. Stir until the chocolate is just melted, then remove from the heat. Beat until smooth and leave the mixture to cool. When cool enough to handle, knead to a smooth paste on a clean work surface. The mixture can now be rolled and cut to shape. If the paste hardens, wrap it in clingfilm and warm it in the microwave for a few seconds on low.

Caramel and Praline Decorations

~ Caramel – To make caramel, put 75 g/3 oz granulated sugar into a heavy-based saucepan with about 3 tablespoons cold water.

Over a low heat, stir well until the sugar has dissolved completely. If any sugar clings to the pan, brush it down using a wet brush. Bring the mixture to the boil and cook, without stirring, until the mixture turns golden. You may need to tilt the pan carefully to ensure the sugar colours evenly. As soon as the desired colour is reached, remove the pan from the heat and plunge the base of the pan into cold water to stop it from cooking further.

๛ Praline – To make praline, follow the instructions as for caramel, but during the final stage, do not plunge the pan into cold water. Add nuts to the caramel mixture, do not stir, but pour immediately onto an oiled baking sheet. Leave to set at room temperature. Once cold, the praline can be chopped or broken into pieces as required. Keep leftover praline in a sealed container. It will keep for several months if stored this way.

๛ Caramel-dipped Nuts – For caramel-dipped nuts, make the caramel, remove the pan from the heat and plunge into cold water as described earlier. Using two skewers or two forks, dip individual nuts into the hot caramel, lift out carefully, allowing excess to run off, then transfer to a foil-covered tray to set. If the caramel becomes too sticky or starts making a lot of sugar strands, reheat gently until liquid again.

๛ Caramel Shapes – For caramel shapes, make the caramel, remove the pan from the heat and plunge into cold water as described earlier. Using a teaspoon, drizzle or pour spoonfuls of caramel onto an oiled baking sheet. Leave to set before removing from the baking sheet. Do not refrigerate as the shapes will liquefy.

๛ Caramel Lace – To make caramel lace, follow the method for caramel shapes, but use the teaspoon to drizzle threads in a random pattern onto an oiled tray. When set, break into pieces to use as decoration. Do not refrigerate.

Handling Chocolate

Icing Recipes

Cream Cheese Frosting

Covers a 20 cm/8 in round cake or 12 cupcakes

50 g/2 oz unsalted butter, softened
300 g/11 oz icing sugar, sifted
flavouring of choice
food colourings
125 g/4 oz cream cheese

Beat the butter and icing sugar together until light and
fluffy. Add the flavourings and colourings of choice and
beat again. Add the cream cheese and whisk until light
and fluffy. Do not overbeat, however, or the mixture can
become runny.

Basic Buttercream

Covers a 20 cm/8 in round cake or 12 cupcakes

150 g/5 oz unsalted butter, softened
225 g/8 oz icing sugar, sifted
2 tbsp hot milk or water
1 tsp vanilla extract
food colourings of choice

Beat the butter until light and fluffy, then beat in the sifted icing sugar and hot milk or water in two batches. Add the vanilla extract and any food colourings. Store chilled for up to 2 days in a lidded container.

Royal Icing

Covers a 20 cm/8 in round cake or 12 cupcakes

2 medium egg whites
500 g/1 lb 1 oz icing sugar, sifted
2 tsp lemon juice

Put the egg whites in a large bowl and whisk lightly with a fork to break up the whites until foamy. Sift in half the icing sugar with the lemon juice and beat well with an electric mixer for 4 minutes, or by hand with a wooden spoon for about 10 minutes until smooth.

Gradually sift in the remaining icing sugar and beat again until thick, smooth and brilliant white and the icing forms soft peaks when flicked up with a spoon. Keep the royal icing covered with a clean damp cloth until you are ready to use it, or store in the refrigerator in a tightly lidded plastic container until needed. If making royal icing ahead of time to use later, beat it again before use to remove any air bubbles that may have formed in the mixture.

Glacé Icing

Covers a 20 cm/8 in round cake or 12 cupcakes

225 g/8 oz icing sugar
few drops lemon juice, or vanilla or almond extract
2–3 tbsp boiling water
liquid food colouring

Icing Recipes

Sift the icing sugar into a bowl and add the chosen flavouring. Gradually stir in enough water to mix to a consistency of thick cream. Beat with a wooden spoon until the icing is thick enough to coat the back of the spoon. Add colouring, if liked, and use at once, because the icing will begin to form a skin.

Apricot Glaze

Covers two 20 cm/8 in round cakes or 24 cupcakes

450 g/1 lb apricot jam
3 tbsp water
1 tsp lemon juice

Place the jam, water and juice in a heavy-based saucepan and heat gently, stirring, until soft and melted. Boil rapidly for 1 minute, then press through a fine sieve with the back of a wooden spoon. Discard the pieces of fruit. Use immediately for glazing or sticking on almond paste and/or fondant, or pour into a clean jar or plastic container, seal and refrigerate for up to 3 months.

Almond Paste

Covers two 20 cm/8 in round cakes or 24 cupcakes

125 g/4 oz icing sugar, sifted
125 g/4 oz caster sugar
225 g/8 oz ground almonds
1 medium egg
1 tsp lemon juice

Stir the sugars and ground almonds together in a bowl. Whisk the egg and lemon juice together and mix into the dry ingredients. Knead until the paste is smooth. Wrap tightly in clingfilm or foil and store in the refrigerator until needed. The paste can be made 2–3 days ahead of time, but after that it will start to dry out and become difficult to handle.

To use the almond paste, knead on a surface lightly dusted with icing sugar until soft and pliable. Brush the top of each cake with apricot glaze. Roll out the paste and cut out discs to cover the tops of the cakes. Press onto the cakes. (*See* page 45 for covering a large cake.)

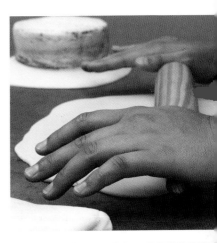

Rolling Fondant (Sugarpaste)

Covers a 20 cm/8 in round cake or 12 cupcakes, or use for decorations

1 medium egg white
1 tbsp liquid glucose
350 g/12 oz icing sugar, sifted

Place the egg white and liquid glucose in a large mixing bowl and stir together with a fork, breaking up the egg white. Add the icing sugar gradually, mixing in with a palette knife, until the mixture binds together and forms a ball. Turn the ball of fondant out onto a clean surface dusted with icing sugar and knead for 5 minutes until soft but firm enough to roll out. If the icing is too soft, knead in a little more icing sugar until the mixture is pliable.

To colour, knead in paste food colouring. Do not use liquid food colouring, because this is not suitable and will make the fondant go limp.

To use, roll out thinly on a clean surface dusted with icing sugar and cut out discs or shapes to cover cakes, on top of almond paste or buttercream, if liked. Or mould into three-dimensional shapes and leave to dry for 24 hours in egg cartons lined with clingfilm.

Icing Recipes

Flower Paste

Ingredients

2 tsp powdered gelatine
2 tsp liquid glucose
2 tsp white vegetable fat
450 g/1 lb sifted icing sugar
1 tsp gum tragacanth powder
1 egg white

Flower, petal or 'gum' paste is used for making very thin, delicate flowers and decorations, which set hard so that they can be handled easily.

Flower paste will roll out much more thinly than sugarpaste and is worth using for wedding cakes, as it gives a realistic finish to flowers, and these can be made ahead of time and easily stored. It can be bought from cake decorating suppliers or by mail order in small, ready-made slabs in different colours or as a powder that can be reconstituted with a little cold water and made into a paste.

To make your own, follow the recipe and store the paste in the refrigerator, tightly wrapped in strong plastic until needed.

Place 1^1/$_2$ tsp cold water in a heatproof bowl. Sprinkle over the gelatine and add the liquid glucose and white fat. Place the bowl over a saucepan of hot water and heat until melted, stirring occasionally. Cool slightly.

Sift the icing sugar and gum tragacanth powder into a bowl, make a well in the centre and add the egg white and the cooled gelatine mixture. Mix together to make a soft paste. Knead the paste on a surface dusted with icing sugar until smooth, then wrap in clingfilm to exclude all air. Leave for 2 hours, then break off small pieces and use to make fine flowers and petals.

Using Icings

Covering a Cake with Almond Paste

Almond paste (*see* page 42) gives a base layer over which to cover a cake with icing, giving a smooth, flat surface that encloses the cake and keeps it moist. Rich fruit cakes need to be covered in almond paste to cover the dark cake and improve its keeping qualities.

First, remove all the papers in which the cake was baked, and trim the top of the cake level if it has peaked. Brush the top and sides of the cake with apricot glaze (*see* page 42).

Sprinkle a clean flat surface with icing sugar and knead one third of the almond paste. Roll out to the same shape as the top of the cake and lay the paste on top.

Measure the circumference of the cake or the length of one side with a piece of string. Knead the remaining paste and, using the string as a guide, roll the paste into a strip long enough to go round the cake and wide enough to cover the sides. Roll the paste up into a coil and press one end onto the side of the cake. Unroll the paste, pressing into the sides of the cake as you go round. Press the top and sides together to join them.

Flatten the top and sides with a small rolling pin or an icing smoother and leave to dry out for 24 hours before icing and decorating.

Using Buttercream and Cream Cheese Frostings

These soft icings can be swirled onto the tops of cakes with a small palette knife or placed in a piping bag fitted with a star nozzle to pipe impressive whirls, such as when you want to finish off your cake with a piped border or simply add those elegant flourishes.

Keep cakes with frostings in a cool place, or refrigerate, as they contain a high percentage of butter, which will melt easily in too warm a place.

❧ Covering a Cake with Frosting – Do not be mean with the amount of frosting you use. If this is scraped on thinly, you will see the cake underneath, so be generous.

If your cake has a dark crumb base, such as a chocolate cake, place it in the freezer for 15 minutes before spreading over the buttercream, to give a firm base that will keep the crumbs from spreading into the buttercream.

Place a generous amount in the centre of the cake and spread this over the top with a large, flat-bladed knife or a palette knife. Spread over the sides separately and tidy up the edges with an icing scraper.

❧ Piping Buttercream onto Cupcakes – Take a large piping bag and add the nozzle of your choice. A star nozzle will give a whirly effect and a plain nozzle will create a smooth coiled effect. Half fill the bag, shake down the buttercream and fill the bag again.

Twist the top round to seal tightly. Squeeze the bag until the buttercream comes out. Start on the outer edge and gently squeeze the buttercream out in one continuous spiral. Lift the bag away to give a peaked finish to the top.

ço **Decorating Buttercream** – Cakes coated in buttercream can be decorated easily with colourful sprinkles and sugars. This is easy with cupcakes. Place the sprinkles in a small saucer or on a piece of nonstick baking parchment and roll the outside edges of each cupcake in the decorations.

Using Sugarpaste

Sugarpaste is a versatile icing, as it can be used for covering whole cakes or modelling all sorts of fancy decorations.

ço Paste food colourings are best for working with sugarpaste and a little goes a very long way. As these are very concentrated, use a cocktail stick to add dots of paste gradually, until you are sure of the colour, and knead in until even (*see* right).

ço Always roll out almond paste or sugarpaste on a surface lightly dusted with icing sugar. Use cornflour for rolling out flower paste as this needs to be kept dry and flexible.

ço **To Make Roses** – Take a small piece of sugarpaste and make a small cone shape, then roll a small pea-size piece into a ball. Flatten out the ball into a petal shape and wrap this round the cone shape.

Continue adding more petals, then trim the thick base. Leave to dry for 2 hours in a clean egg box lined with foil or clingfilm.

Using Icing

~ Covering a Large Cake with Sugarpaste Icing – If covered in almond paste, brush the paste lightly with a little boiled water, or, if using buttercream or apricot glaze, spread these over the trimmed cake to give a surface for the sugarpaste to stick to.

Knead the sugarpaste until softened, then roll into a ball. Roll out to about 1 cm/^{1}/$_2$ inch thickness on a flat surface lightly dusted with icing sugar, moving the sugarpaste occasionally to prevent it from sticking to the surface.

Take a piece of string and measure the distance across the top and down either side of the cake and cut the sugarpaste 2.5 cm/1 inch larger in order to cover the whole cake. Lift the sugarpaste carefully onto the cake, holding it flat with your palms until it is central.

Dust your hands with icing sugar and smooth the icing down over the top and sides of the cake, fluting out the bottom edges. Do not pleat the icing, as this will leave lines. Smooth down to remove any air bubbles under the surface of the icing, then trim the edges with a sharp knife.

Using the flat of your hand or an icing smoother, flatten out the top and sides using a circular movement. Do not wear any rings, as these will leave ridges in the soft icing. Gather up the trimmings into a ball and keep these tightly wrapped in a plastic bag.

~ To Cover Cupcakes – Cut out circles the size of the cupcake tops. Coat each cake with a little apricot glaze or buttercream and press on the circles to form a flat surface.

Leave sugarpaste-covered cakes to firm up for 2 hours before adding decorations, as this provides a good finished surface to work on. Once decorated, store sugarpaste-covered cakes in large boxes in a cool place. Do not store in a refrigerator, as the sugarpaste will become damp and colours may run.

Using Royal Icing

⚬ **Covering a Cake with Royal Icing** – Make sure the almond paste has dried out for 24 hours, or oil from the paste may seep into the icing. Place a large spoonful of icing in the centre of the cake and smooth out using a palette knife in a paddling movement to get rid of any air bubbles.

Draw an icing rule across the top of the cake towards you at an angle. Repeat, pulling back and forth, until the icing is flat. Remove any surplus icing round the top edges and leave to dry out for 24 hours. Keep the remaining icing covered in an airtight plastic box. To cover the sides, for best results, place the cake on an icing turntable. Spread a layer of icing round the sides, using the same paddling motion. Smooth the surface roughly, then, holding an icing scraper at a 45-degree angle, rotate the cake, keeping the scraper still. Rotate the cake until the sides are flat, then carefully lift away any excess icing with a palette knife to give a clean top edge. Leave to dry out for 24 hours. Repeat, adding another layer of icing to give a smooth surface for decorating.

⚬ **Piping Royal Icing Borders** – Fit a small paper icing bag with a star or a straight nozzle and fill the bag three-quarters full with royal icing. Fold over the top and push out a little of the icing at right angles to the base of the cake. As the icing is pushed out, reduce the pressure and lift the bag away. Continue piping another shape next to the first one, until you have completed the border round the base of the cake. You can use the same technique for piping buttercream onto cakes, but this will be a little softer to pipe out and requires less pressure.

Using Icing

∾ Piping Flowers on a Flower Nail – Cut small squares of waxed paper and attach each to a flower nail with a dot of royal icing.

To pipe a rose, half fill a small piping bag fitted with a flower nozzle and, holding the nozzle with the thinnest part uppermost, pipe a small cone onto the paper to form the rosebud. Pipe petals round the rosebud onto the paper, overlapping each one and curling the edge away. Leave the roses to dry out for 12 hours, then peel away from the paper to use, or store in an airtight container between layers of baking parchment until needed.

To pipe a daisy, work with the thick edge of the nozzle towards the centre and pipe five even-sized petals so that they meet in a star shape. Pipe a round dot in the centre in a contrasting colour and leave to dry out as above.

Using Glacé Icing

A quick and easy way to cover cakes and cookies is by using glacé icing. This is just a paste made from icing sugar and water until a coating consistency is formed. Liquid or paste food colourings can be added to glacé and it needs to be used immediately, as it will start to set once spread. Add any sprinkles or decorations to the wet glacé icing immediately, or sprinkle over chopped nuts or cherries.

To make a feathered effect in glacé icing, colour one batch of icing, then colour a little icing in a contrasting colour and place this in a small paper icing bag. Spread the main colour over the cake or cookie and then pipe a pattern onto the wet icing and pull a wooden toothpick through this immediately to give a feathered effect. Work quickly while the icing is wet and then leave to dry and set for 1 hour.

Stacking Tiered Cakes

For large tiered cakes, you will need to insert small sticks of wooden or plastic dowelling into the lower tiers to take the weight of the next layer and stop it sinking.

First decide where you need to position the dowels: cover the cake with almond paste and sugarpaste and place centrally on a board. Place a sheet of baking parchment over the cake, cut to the size of the top of the cake. Based on the size of the cake that is to stand on top, decide where you want the dowels to go and mark four equal dots in a square, centrally on the paper.

Replace the paper and mark through each dot with a skewer. Remove the paper and push a dowel down into the cake at each mark. Make a mark with a pencil on the dowel at the point where the dowel comes out of the cake. Pull the dowels out of the cake and, using a serrated knife, trim them to 1 mm/^{1}/$_{32}$ inch above the pencil mark. Replace the dowels in the cake and ensure these are all 1 mm above the surface of the cake. If not, trim them again, then place the next tier of the cake on top (this should be sitting on a thin cake board that fits its size). Repeat if using three tiers.

If you are going to transport a tiered cake, remember to take each tier in a separate cardboard cake box and assemble it at the venue. Do not ever think of trying to transport a tiered cake once it is stacked up – it will be too heavy and you may damage all your hard work.

Using Icing

Seasonal

Celebration

Cakes

Whether it's the dead of winter or the height of summer, a cake is always appreciated! Make everyone remember a seasonal celebration with an extra special cake. The Cute Critters Easter Cupcakes will be sure to delight anybody, not just the children, and any mother would appreciate a Mother's Day Bouquet Cake. The Christmas Cranberry Chocolate Log is a wonderful new twist on the traditional roulade.

Valentine Heart Cupcakes

Makes 12

150 g/5 oz butter, softened
150 g/5 oz caster sugar
3 medium eggs, beaten
1 tsp vanilla extract
2 tbsp milk
225 g/8 oz ready-to-roll sugarpaste
icing sugar, for dusting
1 batch cream cheese frosting

Preheat the oven to 180°C/350°F/Gas Mark 4 and line a 12-hole tray with deep paper cases.

Place the butter, sugar, eggs, vanilla extract and milk in a bowl, then sift in the flour and baking powder. Beat together for about 2 minutes with an electric hand-mixer until pale and fluffy. Spoon into the paper cases and bake for 20–25 minutes until firm and golden. Cool on a wire rack.

To decorate, colour one third of the sugarpaste pink and one third red, leaving the rest white. Dust a clean, flat surface with icing sugar. Roll out the sugarpaste thinly and, using a cutter or the template on page 250, cut out pink, red and white heart shapes, then leave to dry flat and harden for 2 hours. Colour the cream cheese frosting pale pink and place in a piping bag fitted with a star nozzle.

Pipe a swirl on top of each cupcake and decorate with the hearts. Keep in a cool place for up to 2 days.

Mother's Day Bouquet Cake

Serves 12–14

For the cake base:

1 x 20 cm/8 inch round Madeira cake
(*see* page 29)
3 tbsp sieved apricot jam

To decorate:

1.25 kg/2^1/$_4$ lb ready-to-roll
sugarpaste icing
icing sugar, for dusting
pink and green paste food colours

Trim the top of the cake flat if it has peaked and brush the jam over the top and sides of the cake. Cover the cake with 550 g/1^1/$_4$ lb sugarpaste and place on a 25 cm/10 inch cake board or flat serving plate.

Colour 350 g/12 oz sugarpaste pink and 125 g/4 oz green. Roll 175 g/ 6 oz pink sugarpaste out on a surface lightly dusted with icing sugar to a long thin strip, 5 cm/2 inches wide x 68.5 cm/27 inches long. Dampen the underside of the ribbon by lightly brushing with a little cold boiled water. Roll the strip carefully round the outside of the cake and press the join to neaten. Keep the join at the back of the cake.

Model the remaining pink sugarpaste into 8 roses (*see* page 47) and leave these for 2–3 hours in egg boxes lined with crumped foil until firm.

Using the green sugarpaste, cut out 10 leaves and mark veins on them using a sharp knife. Roll scraps of green sugarpaste into long thin sausages. Lightly dampen the underside of the roses and leaves and arrange at the back of the cake in a semi-circle with the leaves and green stems.

Mother's Day Rose Cupcakes

Makes 12

125 g/4 oz caster sugar
125 g/4 oz soft tub margarine
2 medium eggs
125 g/4 oz self-raising flour
1 tsp baking powder
1 tsp rosewater

To decorate:

50 g/2 oz ready-to-roll sugarpaste
pink paste food colouring
350 g/12 oz fondant
icing sugar

Preheat the oven to 190˚C/375˚F/Gas Mark 5. Line a 12-hole bun tray with paper cases.

Place all the cupcake ingredients in a large bowl and beat with an electric mixer for about 2 minutes until smooth. Fill the paper cases halfway up with the mixture. Bake for about 15 minutes until firm, risen and golden. Remove to a wire rack to cool.

To decorate the cupcakes, first line an egg box with foil and set aside. Colour the sugarpaste with pink paste food colouring. Make a small cone shape, then roll a pea-sized piece of sugarpaste into a ball. Flatten out the ball into a petal shape and wrap this round the cone shape. Continue adding more petals to make a rose, then trim the thick base, place in the egg box and leave to dry out for 2 hours.

Blend the fondant icing sugar with a little water to make a thick icing of spreading consistency, then colour this pale pink. Smooth over the top of each cupcake and decorate with the roses immediately. Leave to set for 1 hour. Keep for 1 day in an airtight container.

Easter Egg Cake Pops

Makes 12

For the unbaked cake pops:

350 g/12 oz leftover or bought
Madeira cake
175 g/6 oz white or milk
chocolate, melted

To decorate:

$^1/_2$ batch vanilla buttercream
700 g/1$^1/_2$ lb ready-to-roll sugarpaste
pink, yellow, blue, orange and green
paste food colourings
12 thin lollipop sticks
block floristry foam
$^1/_2$ batch royal icing
(*see* page 41)

Chop the Madeira cake and crumble into fine crumbs in a bowl. Pour in the melted chocolate and stir with your hands to a stiff mixture, then mould into twelve balls. Place on a tray and chill in the refrigerator for 2 hours until firm.

Take each cake pop and roll it lightly between your palms to make an oval shape. Coat each cake pop thickly in buttercream, then place on a baking tray.

Divide the sugarpaste into 12 pieces and colour three pink, three yellow and three blue. Take a pink piece of sugarpaste and roll this into a ball. Using a small plastic rolling pin, roll the ball out to a circle large enough to cover the oval shape. Drape the sugarpaste over the oval shape, trim and press the joins together until smooth. Roll the oval between your palms to make a smooth finish. Repeat the covering and rolling process until all the ovals are covered, then place them on the lollipop sticks and place them in the floristry foam to keep them secure and upright.

Divide the royal icing into four batches and colour orange, light blue, yellow and leave one batch white. Place each batch in a small paper icing bag fitted with a no 1 plain nozzle and pipe on wiggly lines, hearts, daisies and small blossom flowers as shown (or use sugarpaste if you prefer).

Easter Nest Cupcakes

Makes 12

125 g/4 oz soft margarine
125 g/4 oz golden caster sugar
150 g/5 oz self-raising flour
2 tbsp cocoa powder
2 medium eggs
1 tbsp golden syrup

To decorate:

1 batch buttercream
(see page 40)
50 g/2 oz shredded wheat cereal
125 g/4 oz milk chocolate,
broken into pieces
25 g/1 oz unsalted butter
chocolate mini eggs

Preheat the oven to 180°C/350°F/Gas Mark 4. Line a 12-hole bun tray with paper cases.

Place the margarine and the sugar in a large bowl, then sift in the flour and cocoa powder. In another bowl, beat the eggs with the syrup, then add to the first bowl. Whisk together with an electric beater for 2 minutes, or by hand with a wooden spoon until smooth.

Divide the mixture between the cases, filling them three-quarters full. Bake for about 15 minutes until they are springy to the touch in the centre. Turn out to cool on a wire rack.

To decorate, swirl the buttercream over the top of each cupcake. Break up the shredded wheat finely. Melt the chocolate with the butter, then stir in the shredded wheat and let cool slightly. Line a plate with clingfilm. Mould the mixture into tiny nest shapes with your fingers, then place them on the lined plate. Freeze for a few minutes to harden. Set a nest on top of each cupcake and fill with mini eggs. Keep for 2 days in a cool place in an airtight container.

Simnel Easter Muffins

Makes 6–8

125 g/4 oz yellow marzipan
150 ml/¹/₄ pint milk
50 g/2 oz soft light brown sugar
2 medium eggs
175 g/6 oz self-raising flour
¹/₂ tsp mixed spice
75 g/3 oz mixed dried fruit
50 g/2 oz glacé cherries,
washed and chopped
75 g/3 oz butter,
melted and cooled

Preheat the oven to 190°C/375°F/Gas Mark 5. Line a deep muffin tray with six to eight paper cases, depending on the depth of the holes. Weigh 25 g/1 oz of the marzipan and roll into long thin strips. Grate or chop the remaining marzipan into small chunks.

Whisk the milk, sugar and eggs together in a jug. Sift the flour and spice into a bowl, then stir together with the fruit, cherries and the marzipan chunks. Pour the milk mixture into the flour mixture along with the melted butter. Mix until combined.

Spoon into the paper cases and make a cross over the top of each using two marzipan strips. Bake for about 20 minutes until firm in the centre. Cool in the tins for 3 minutes, then turn out to cool on a wire rack. Eat warm or cold. Keep for 24 hours sealed in an airtight container.

Cute Critters Easter Cupcakes

Makes 12

For the cakes:

1 batch vanilla cupcakes
(*see* page 31)

To decorate:

450 g/1 lb ready-to-roll sugarpaste
pink, orange, blue, yellow, green and
mauve paste food colourings
icing sugar, for dusting
1 batch vanilla buttercream
tiny edible metallic balls
2 tbsp royal icing (*see* page 41), or a
small tube of royal icing

Colour 25 g/1 oz sugarpaste deep pink, 50 g/2 oz light pink, 25 g/1 oz orange, 50 g/2 oz blue, 50 g/2 oz yellow, 25 g/1 oz green and 25 g/1 oz mauve and leave the remainder white. Roll out the deep pink paste on a board or surface dusted with icing sugar and cut out 12 daisies using a medium daisy stamp. Repeat with the white sugarpaste, using a larger daisy and stamp out 12 white daisies. Roll the orange sugarpaste into 24 small carrot shapes. Mould the light pink sugarpaste into four pink rabbits and repeat with the blue sugarpaste, making four blue rabbits. Model the yellow sugarpaste into four chicks. Roll scraps into small ovals for tiny eggs and make coloured centres for the daisies from scraps. Leave all the pieces to dry for 1 hour on nonstick baking parchment.

Trim the tops of the cakes flat if they have peaked. Colour the buttercream pale green and place in a piping bag fitted with a star nozzle. Pipe a thick swirl onto the top of each cupcake, then arrange a pink and white daisy and two carrots on each cake. Make carrot tops from small green strips of sugarpaste. Place the chicks on four cakes and repeat with the blue and pink rabbits. Make beaks for the chicks. Press metallic balls on the animals for eyes and decorate the rabbits' faces with royal icing as shown. Arrange the eggs on the cakes in batches of three to finish.

Father's Day Cupcakes

Makes 14

125 g/4 oz self-raising flour
125 g/4 oz caster sugar
125 g/4 oz soft margarine
2 medium eggs, beaten
1 tsp vanilla extract

To decorate:

1 batch buttercream
(see page 40)
blue, yellow and orange paste
food colourings
225 g/8 oz ready-to-roll sugarpaste
50 g/2 oz royal icing sugar
edible silver balls

Preheat the oven to 180°C/350°F/Gas Mark 4. Line two 12-hole bun trays with 14 paper fairy-cake cases or silicone moulds.

Sift the flour into a bowl and stir together with the caster sugar. Add the margarine, eggs and vanilla extract and beat together for about 2 minutes until smooth. Spoon into the cases and bake for 15–20 minutes until golden and firm to the touch. Turn out on a wire rack. When cool, trim the tops flat if they have peaked slightly.

To decorate, colour half the buttercream yellow and the other half orange and swirl over the top of each cupcake. Dust a clean, flat surface with icing sugar. Colour the sugarpaste light blue and roll out thinly. Stamp or cut out large stars 4 cm/1$^{1}/_{2}$ inches wide and place these on the buttercream. Make up the royal icing mix and place in a paper piping bag with the end snipped away and pipe 'Dad' or names on the stars. Decorate with the edible silver balls. Keep for 3 days in an airtight container.

Witch's Hat Halloween Cupcakes

Makes 12

For the cakes:

1 batch chocolate cupcakes
(*see* page 31)

To decorate:

1 batch cream cheese frosting
(*see* page 40)
orange, yellow and black paste
food colourings
450 g/1 lb ready-to-roll sugarpaste
black sugar sprinkles

Colour the cream cheese frosting bright orange with a little paste food colouring and place in a piping bag fitted with a star nozzle. Pipe a large swirl on top of each cake.

Colour 40 g/1^1/$_2$ oz sugarpaste orange and 15 g/^{1}/$_2$ oz yellow. Colour the remaining sugarpaste black. To model the witch's hats, divide the black sugarpaste into 12 equal pieces. Roll each piece into a pointed cone, curve the top over, then pinch out the base between your fingers to form a flat edge.

Place the hats on a sheet of nonstick baking parchment. Roll the orange sugarpaste into a thin sausage, then roll with a small rolling pin to flatten this out. Cut into 12 lengths, each long enough to fit round the base of a hat.

Dampen the underside of each strip lightly with cold boiled water and stick around the hats. Roll out the yellow sugarpaste thinly and cut into 12 small squares. Cut out the centre of each square and very carefully stick the yellow buckle onto the hat trim. Place the hats on the orange frosting just before serving and scatter over the black sugar sprinkles.

Halloween Mice Cake

Serves 10–12

For the cake base:

1 batch 20 cm/8 inch, round
rich chocolate cake mix (*see*
page 28) baked in two 1.1 litre/
2 pint heatproof basins for
40 minutes, or until a skewer
pressed into the centre of each
cake comes out clean

To decorate:

1 batch chocolate buttercream
(*see* page 40)
700 g/1¹/₂ lb ready-to-roll sugarpaste
orange, green and brown paste
food colourings
icing sugar, for dusting
black sugarcraft icing pen

Trim the tops of the cakes level if they have peaked and sandwich them
together with some of the buttercream to make a ball. Spread the remaining
buttercream over the outside of the cake.

Colour 400 g/14 oz sugarpaste orange and use to cover the cake (*see* page
48). Mark ridges down the sides with the handle of a wooden spoon to give
a realistic pumpkin shape. Colour half the remaining sugarpaste green and
shape a stalk. Dampen the base of this and press on top of the cake. Roll
out small pieces of the paste and cut out two leaves with a sharp knife or leaf
cutter. Mark veins on the leaves with a knife, dampen them and press onto
the lower part of the cake at the front and the back. Roll two long, thin, green
sausages, dampen and press onto the front and back of the cake, looping as
shown, from the stalk to the leaves.

Cut two holes in the sugarpaste either side of the stalk, for the mice's heads to
poke out, and holes beneath for their tails. Reserve a very tiny piece of white
sugarpaste to make eyes for the mice and colour the rest light brown. Shape
the heads of the mice and press two tiny white eyes on each. Push a cocktail
stick into each of the higher holes in the cake and press a mouse head onto it.
Shape ears and feet out of the remaining brown sugarpaste, then dampen
and press into place. Mark smiling mouths with the point of a sharp knife and
draw pupils onto the eyes with a black sugarcraft pen. Add a small orange
sugarpaste nose to one mouse, fixing it in place with a dab of cold boiled water.
Shape two tails from brown sugarpaste, dampen and press on as shown.

Winter Cupcakes

Makes 12–14

125 g/4 oz butter
125 g/4 oz soft dark muscovado sugar
2 medium eggs, beaten
225 g/8 oz self-raising flour
1 tsp ground mixed spice
finely grated zest and 1 tbsp juice
from 1 orange
1 tbsp black treacle
350 g/12 oz mixed dried fruit

To decorate:

3 tbsp sieved apricot glaze
(see page 42)
450 g/1 lb almond paste
(see page 42)
icing sugar, for dusting
225 g/8 oz ready-to-roll sugarpaste
225 g/8 oz royal icing
fancy paper wrappers (optional)

Preheat the oven to 180°C/350°F/Gas Mark 4. Line one or two 12-hole trays with 12–14 deep paper cases. Beat the butter and sugar together until light and fluffy, then beat in the eggs a little at a time, adding 1 teaspoon flour with each addition. Sift in the remaining flour and the spice, add the orange zest and juice, the treacle and dried fruit to the bowl and fold together until the mixture is blended. Spoon into the trays and bake for 30 minutes. Leave to cool in the trays for 15 minutes, then turn out onto a wire rack. Store undecorated in an airtight container for up to 3 weeks, or freeze until needed.

To decorate the cupcakes, trim the top of each cake level, then brush with apricot glaze. Roll out the almond paste and cut out eight discs 6 cm/2^1/$_2$ inches wide. Place these over the glaze and press level. Leave to dry for 24 hours. Dust a clean, flat surface with icing sugar. Roll out the sugarpaste and stamp or cut out holly leaf and ivy shapes. Leave to dry for 2 hours. Swirl the royal icing over the top of each cupcake. Press in the holly and ivy shapes and leave to set for 2 hours. Once decorated, keep in an airtight container for 3 days.

Festive Candy Cane Cupcakes

Makes 14–18

150 g/5 oz butter, softened
150 g/5 oz caster sugar
150 g/5 oz self-raising flour
25 g/1 oz ground almonds
3 medium eggs, beaten
1 tsp vanilla extract
2 tbsp milk

To decorate:

225 g/8 oz sugarpaste
red and green paste
food colourings
450 g/1 lb royal icing sugar

Preheat the oven to 180°C/350°F/Gas Mark 4. Line two 12-hole bun trays with 14–18 foil cases, depending on the depth of the holes. Place the butter and sugar in a bowl, sift in the flour and stir in the almonds. Add the eggs to the bowl along with the vanilla extract and milk. Spoon into the cases, filling them three-quarters full. Bake for about 18 minutes until firm to the touch in the centre. Turn out onto a wire rack. Once cool, trim the tops if peaked.

To decorate, colour one quarter of the sugarpaste red and one quarter green. Dust a clean, flat surface with icing sugar. Roll out the sugarpaste into long sticks with the palms of your hands. Roll a stick of red with a stick of white to form a twist. Cut into short lengths about 5 cm/2^1/$_2$ inches long and bend to form a cane shape. Leave to dry for 2 hours.

Make up the royal icing according to the packet instructions to a soft icing that will form peaks. Smooth the icing onto the cupcakes and place a cane centrally on each cupcake. Place the remaining icing in a small piping bag fitted with a star nozzle and pipe a star border round the outside of each cupcake. Keep for 2 days in an airtight container.

Christmas Cake

Serves 12–14

900 g/2 lb mixed dried fruit
75 g/3 oz glacé cherries,
rinsed and halved
3 tbsp brandy or orange juice
finely grated zest and juice
of 1 lemon
225 g/8 oz soft dark
muscovado sugar
225 g/8 oz butter,
at room temperature
4 medium eggs, beaten
225 g/8 oz plain flour
1 tbsp black treacle
1 tbsp mixed spice

To decorate:

2–4 tbsp brandy (optional)
4 tbsp sieved apricot jam
700 g/1 1/2 lb almond paste
(see page 42)
icing sugar, for dusting
1 kg/2 lb 3 oz ready-to-roll sugarpaste
bought decorations and ribbon

Place the dried fruit and cherries in a bowl and sprinkle over the brandy or orange juice and the lemon zest and juice. Stir and let soak for 2–4 hours. Preheat the oven to 150°C/300°F/Gas Mark 2. Grease and double-line the base and sides of a 20.5 cm/8 inch round deep cake tin. Beat the sugar and butter together until soft and fluffy. Beat the eggs in gradually, adding 1 teaspoon of flour with each addition. Stir in the treacle, then sift in the rest of the flour and the spice. Add the soaked fruit and stir until the mixture is smooth. Spoon into the tin and smooth the top level. Bake for 1 hour, then reduce the temperature to 140°C/275°F/Gas Mark 1 and bake for a further 2–2 1/2 hours until a skewer inserted into the centre comes out clean. Leave the cake to cool in the tin, then, when completely cold, remove and wrap in greaseproof paper and then in foil and store in a cool place for 1–3 months.

To decorate, brush the cake all over with brandy, if using. Heat the jam and brush over the top and sides. Roll out one third of the almond paste and cut into a disc the size of the top of the cake, using the empty tin as a guide. Place the disc on top. Roll the remaining paste into a strip long enough to cover the sides of the cake and press on. Leave the almond paste to dry out in a cool place for 2 days. On a surface dusted with icing sugar, roll out the sugarpaste to a circle large enough to cover the top and sides of the cake. Brush 1 tablespoon brandy or cold boiled water over the almond paste and place the sugarpaste on top. Smooth down and trim. Make a border from tiny balls of sugarpaste and decorate.

Christmas Cranberry Chocolate Log

Serves 12–14

For the chocolate ganache frosting:
300 ml/$^1/_2$ pint double cream
350 g/12 oz dark chocolate, chopped
2 tbsp brandy (optional)

For the roulade:
5 large eggs, separated
3 tbsp cocoa powder, sifted, plus
extra for dusting
125 g/4 oz icing sugar, sifted, plus
extra for dusting
$^1/_4$ tsp cream of tartar

For the filling:
175 g/6 oz cranberry sauce
1–2 tbsp brandy (optional)
450 ml/$^3/_4$ pint double cream,
whipped to soft peaks

To decorate:
caramelised orange strips
dried cranberries

Preheat the oven to 200°C/400°F/Gas Mark 6. Bring the cream to the boil over a medium heat. Remove from the heat and add all of the chocolate, stirring until melted. Stir in the brandy, if using, and strain into a medium bowl. Cool. Refrigerate for 6–8 hours.

Lightly oil and line a 39 x 26 cm/15$^1/_2$ x 10$^1/_2$ inch Swiss roll tin with nonstick baking parchment. Using an electric whisk, beat the egg yolks until thick and creamy. Slowly beat in the cocoa powder and half the icing sugar and reserve. Whisk the egg whites and cream of tartar into soft peaks. Gradually whisk in the remaining sugar until the mixture is stiff and glossy. Gently fold the yolk mixture into the egg whites. Spread evenly into the tin. Bake in the oven for 15 minutes. Remove and invert onto a sheet of greaseproof paper dusted with cocoa powder. Cut off the crisp edges of the cake, then roll up. Leave on a wire rack until cold.

For the filling, heat the cranberry sauce with the brandy, if using, until warm and spreadable. Unroll the cooled cake and spread with the cranberry sauce. Allow to cool and set. Carefully spoon the whipped cream over the surface and spread to within 2.5 cm/1 inch of the edges. Re-roll the cake. Transfer to a cake plate or tray. Allow the chocolate ganache to soften at room temperature, then beat until soft and of a spreadable consistency. Spread over the roulade and, using a fork, mark the roulade with ridges to resemble tree bark. Dust with icing sugar. Decorate with the caramelised orange strips and dried cranberries and serve.

Sparkly Christmas Cupcakes

Makes 14–18

125 g/4 oz butter, softened
125 g/4 oz soft dark
muscovado sugar
2 medium eggs, beaten
225 g/8 oz self-raising flour
1 tsp ground mixed spice
finely grated zest and 1 tbsp juice
from 1 orange
1 tbsp black treacle
350 g/12 oz mixed dried fruit

To decorate:

3 tbsp sieved apricot glaze
(see page 42)
225 g/8 oz almond paste
(see page 42)
1 batch royal icing
(see page 41)
edible silver balls

Preheat the oven to 180°C/350°F/Gas Mark 4. Line a 12-hole bun tray with 14–18 foil fairy-cake cases, depending on the size of the holes. Beat the butter and sugar together until light and fluffy, then beat in the eggs a little at a time, adding 1 teaspoon flour with each addition. Sift in the remaining flour and spice, add the orange zest and juice, treacle and dried fruit to the bowl and fold together until the mixture is blended. Spoon into the cases and bake for about 30 minutes. Leave to cool in the trays for 15 minutes, then turn out to cool on a wire rack. Store undecorated in an airtight container for up to 3 weeks, or freeze until needed.

To decorate, trim the top of each cake level, if they have peaked, then brush with apricot glaze. Roll out the almond paste and, using the circle on page 252 as a guide, cut out eight circles. Place a disc on top of each cake and press level. Leave to dry for 24 hours if possible.

Swirl the royal icing over the cakes, flicking into peaks with a palette knife. Use silver balls to decorate while the icing is still wet. Leave to dry for 1 hour. Keep for 4 days in an airtight container.

Special Occasion Cakes

What two words go better together than cake and celebration? Take your special occasion to the next level with any one of the exceptional cakes in this section. The Rainbow Layers Birthday Cake and the Chocolate Boxes Cake are especially sure to amaze, as they are unique and showstopping, just as your celebration should be. The Tiered Rose Cake is also beautifully stunning.

New Home Cupcakes

Makes 14

125 g/4 oz self-raising flour
125 g/4 oz caster sugar
125 g/4 oz soft margarine
2 medium eggs, beaten
1 tsp vanilla extract

To decorate:

125 g/4 oz buttercream
(*see* page 60)
450 g/1 lb ready-to-roll sugarpaste
red, brown and yellow paste
food colourings
gel writing icing tubes

Preheat the oven to 180°C/350°F/Gas Mark 4. Line two 12-hole bun trays with 14 paper fairy-cake cases or silicone moulds.

Sift the flour into a bowl and stir together with the caster sugar. Add the margarine, eggs and vanilla extract and beat together for about 2 minutes until smooth. Spoon into the cases and bake for 15–20 minutes until golden and firm to the touch. Turn out on a wire rack. When cool, trim the tops flat if they have peaked slightly.

To decorate, lightly coat the top of each cupcake with a little buttercream. Dust a clean, flat surface with icing sugar. Colour half the sugarpaste a pale lemon yellow and roll it out thinly. Cut out circles 6 cm/2$^1/_2$ inches wide and place these over the buttercream and press to smooth down. Colour half the remaining icing brown and the other half red. Roll out thinly on a dusted surface. Cut out small squares in the brown icing and then measure across and cut out a triangular roof shape in red icing. Press the shapes onto the cupcakes and pipe on doors, windows and roof tiles in white piping icing. Keep for 3 days in an airtight container.

Chocolate Boxes Cake

Serves 20

For the cake base:

1 x 13 cm/5 inch square chocolate
cake (*see* page 28)
1 x 18 cm/7 inch square
chocolate cake

To decorate:

1 batch chocolate buttercream
(*see* page 40)
225 g/8 oz dark chocolate
225 g/8 oz white chocolate
1/2 batch chocolate modelling paste,
using dark plain chocolate
(*see* page 38)

Trim the top of the cakes and spread the buttercream over the top and sides of each cake. Place the small cake on a 13 cm/5 inch square thin cake board and the larger one on an 18 cm/7 inch square board.

Melt the plain and white chocolate in separate bowls. Using a palette knife, thinly spread the chocolate out on separate sheets of nonstick baking parchment. Leave until cold and set hard then, using a sharp knife, cut two squares from the white chocolate large enough to cover the tops of both cakes. Cut thin strips about 2 cm/3/4 inch wide, and the depth of the cake. Lift the strips up carefully off the paper with a small palette knife and press onto the buttercream, using alternate white and dark strips.

Place the smaller cake on top of the larger one at an angle. Melt the rest of the dark chocolate, place in a small piping bag with a plain nozzle and pipe a shell border around the top and base edges of both cakes.

Knead the modelling chocolate lightly until softened. On a surface lightly dusted with icing sugar, thinly roll to a narrow strip, 1 cm/1/2 inches wide. Cut into 14 cm/51/2 inch lengths and pinch the ends together to make loops. Place the loops around spoon handles lined with clingfilm and leave until firm. Place on top of the cake and secure with a little piped melted chocolate.

Celebration Fruit Cake

Serves 12

125 g/4 oz butter or margarine
125 g/4 oz soft dark brown sugar
380 g can crushed pineapple
150 g/5 oz raisins
150 g/5 oz sultanas
125 g/4 oz crystallised ginger, chopped
125 g/4 oz glacé cherries, chopped
125 g/4 oz mixed cut peel
225 g/8 oz self-raising flour
1 tsp bicarbonate of soda
2 tsp mixed spice
1 tsp ground cinnamon
$1/2$ tsp salt
2 large eggs, beaten

For the topping:

100 g/$3^1/2$ oz pecan or walnut halves, lightly toasted
125 g/4 oz varied glacé cherries
100 g/$3^1/2$ oz pitted prunes or dates
2 tbsp clear honey, to decorate

Preheat the oven to 170°C/325°F/Gas Mark 3, 10 minutes before baking. Heat the butter and sugar in a saucepan until the sugar has dissolved, stirring frequently. Add the pineapple and juice, dried fruits and peel. Bring to the boil, simmer for 3 minutes, stirring occasionally, then remove from the heat to cool completely.

Lightly oil and line the base of a 20.5 x 7.5 cm/8 x 3 inch loose-bottomed cake tin with nonstick baking parchment. Sift the flour, bicarbonate of soda, spices and salt into a bowl.

Add the boiled fruit mixture to the flour with the eggs and mix. Spoon into the tin and smooth the top. Bake in the preheated oven for $1^1/4$ hours, or until a skewer inserted into the centre comes out clean. (If the cake is browning too quickly, cover loosely with foil and reduce the oven temperature.)

Remove and cool completely before removing from the tin and discarding the lining paper. Arrange the nuts, cherries and prunes or dates in an attractive pattern on top of the cake. Heat the honey and brush over the topping to glaze.

Alternatively, toss the nuts and fruits in the warm honey and spread evenly over the top of the cake. Cool completely and store in a cake tin for a day or two before serving, to allow the flavours to develop.

Birthday Numbers Cupcakes

Makes 12–14

125 g/4 oz self-raising flour
125 g/4 oz caster sugar
125 g/4 oz soft margarine
2 medium eggs, beaten
1 tsp vanilla extract

To decorate:

225 g/8 oz ready-to-roll sugarpaste
paste food colourings
icing sugar, for dusting
1 batch buttercream (see page 40)
small candles

Preheat the oven to 180°C/350°F/Gas Mark 4. Line one or two 12-hole bun trays with 12–14 paper fairy-cake cases or silicone moulds, depending on the depth of the holes.

Sift the flour into a bowl and stir together with the caster sugar. Add the margarine, eggs and vanilla extract and beat together for about 2 minutes until smooth.

Spoon into the cases and bake for 15–20 minutes until golden and firm to the touch.Turn out on a wire rack. When cool, trim the tops flat if they have peaked slightly.

To decorate, colour batches of sugarpaste in bright colours. Dust a clean surface lightly with icing sugar. Thinly roll each colour of sugarpaste and cut out numbers using a set of cutters. Leave these for 2 hours to dry and harden.

Using a palette knife, spread the buttercream thickly onto the top of each cupcake. Place a small candle into each cupcake and stand the number up against this. Serve within 8 hours as the numbers may start to soften.

Birthday Bunting Cupcakes

Makes 12

For the cakes:

1 batch vanilla cupcakes
(*see* page 21)

To decorate:

500 g/1 lb 1 oz sugarpaste
deep pink and pale pink paste food
colourings
icing sugar, for dusting
$^1/_4$ batch white royal icing
(*see* page 41)
$^1/_2$ batch vanilla buttercream
(*see* page 40)
pink sugarcraft icing pen (optional)
24 tiny and 6 slightly larger pink
sugarpaste flowers

Trim the tops of the cupcakes if they have peaked. Reserve 50 g/2 oz of the sugarpaste. Divide the rest in half and colour one half deep pink. Roll out the deep pink and white sugarpastes separately on a board dusted with icing sugar. Stamp out three circles from each colour to fit the tops of your cakes (about 6 cm/2$^1/_2$ inches across usually). Press the circles on top of six of the cupcakes, fixing them in place with a little white decorating icing. Spoon the buttercream into a piping bag fitted with a star nozzle and pipe a swirl over the top of the six remaining cupcakes.

Colour the reserved sugarpaste pale pink. Roll out the three colours of sugarpastes separately and cut out 18 tiny triangles to make bunting, and six rectangles the same width as the top of the cupcakes and 1 cm/$^1/_2$ inch wide. Fix three bunting triangles to the top of each sugarpaste-covered cupcake with royal icing, with tiny sugarpaste flowers in between. Decorate some of the triangles with tiny piped dots or stripes in decorating icing, piped on using a small piping bag fitted with a fine writing nozzle. Press a pattern round the edges of others with a cocktail stick.

Mark a pattern around the edges of the rectangles using a cocktail stick and press an appropriate message in the centre of each using an embossing tool, or write the message on with a pink sugarcraft pen. Attach a larger sugarpaste flower in a corner of each rectangle with decorating icing. Press a rectangle on top of each buttercream-covered cupcake.

Daisy Birthday Cake

Serves 80–100

For the cake base:

1 each 15 cm/6 inch, 20 cm/8 inch
and 25 cm/10 inch round
Madeira cakes, covered
in almond paste
(*see* pages 29 and 42)

To decorate:

2.25 kg/4³/₄ lb ready-to-roll
sugarpaste
lemon paste food colouring
icing sugar, for dusting
1 batch royal icing
450 g/1 lb flower paste
cornflour, for dusting
white candles

Colour the sugarpaste pale lemon and divide into 1 kg/2¹/₄ lb, 700 g/1¹/₂ lb and 450 g/1 lb batches. Knead the largest batch until soft, then roll out on a surface lightly dusted with icing sugar to a circle large enough to cover the top and sides of the largest cake. Use to cover the cake as per the instructions on page 48. Repeat, covering the medium and small cakes.

Place the large cake on a 35 cm/14 inch round cake drum, the medium cake on a thin, 20 cm/8 inch round board and the small cake on a thin, 15 cm/6 inch cake board. Stack the cakes on top of each other using dowels as per the instructions on page 51.

Colour three quarters of the royal icing pale yellow and place in a piping bag fitted with a medium plain nozzle. Pipe a rope border around the base of each cake and leave to dry for 24 hours. Reserve the remaining icing.

Colour one third of the flower paste pale yellow for the flower centres. Roll out the white flower paste very thinly on a surface dusted with cornflour. Using a fine large daisy cutter, stamp out a daisy shape, then flute this up to flick out the petals. Roll a tiny ball of yellow paste, flatten out, then mark with a skewer to make the centre of the daisy. Press onto the middle of the petals and leave to dry for 24 hours on nonstick baking parchment. Make eight large, 16 medium and 30 small daisies. When firm, stick to the top and sides of the cakes with the remaining royal icing as shown. Press candles into the top of the cake to finish.

Giftwrapped Presents Cupcakes

Makes 12–14

125 g/4 oz butter
125 g/4 oz soft dark
muscovado sugar
2 medium eggs, beaten
225 g/8 oz self-raising flour
1 tsp ground mixed spice
finely grated zest and 1 tbsp juice
from 1 orange
1 tbsp black treacle
350 g/12 oz mixed dried fruit

To decorate:

3 tbsp sieved apricot glaze
(see page 42)
icing sugar, for dusting
600 g/1 lb 5 oz ready-to-roll
sugarpaste
red, blue, green and yellow paste
food colourings

Preheat the oven to 180°C/350°F/Gas Mark 4. Line one or two 12-hole trays with 12–14 deep paper cases, depending on the depth of the holes. Beat the butter and sugar together until light and fluffy, then beat in the eggs a little at a time, adding 1 teaspoon flour with each addition. Sift in the remaining flour and spice, add the orange zest and juice, treacle and dried fruit to the bowl and fold together until the mixture is blended. Spoon into the cases and bake for about 30 minutes until firm in the centre and a skewer comes out clean. Leave to cool in the trays for 15 minutes, then turn out to cool on a wire rack. Store undecorated in an airtight container for up to 4 weeks, or freeze.

To decorate, trim the top of each cupcake level, then brush with apricot glaze. Dust a clean, flat surface with icing sugar. Colour the sugarpaste in batches and roll out thinly. Cut out circles 6 cm/2¹/2 inches wide. Place a disc on top of each cupcake and press level. Mould coloured scraps into long, thin sticks and roll these out thinly. Place a contrasting colour across each cupcake and arrange into bows and loops. Leave to dry for 24 hours. Keep for 4 days in an airtight container.

Rainbow Layers Birthday Cake

C

Serves 18

For the cake base:

3 batches all-in-one quick-mix
sponge batter (*see page 32*)
red, orange, yellow, green, blue
and purple paste food colourings

To decorate:

2 batches vanilla buttercream
(*see page 40*)
225 g/8 oz ready-to-roll sugarpaste
coloured sprinkles
icing sugar, for dusting

Line two 20 cm/8 inch, round sandwich tins with nonstick baking parchment. Take one batch of quick-mix sponge batter, halve the mixture and colour one half red and one half orange, adding enough food colouring to give a deep tone. Bake following the instructions on page 33–34, then turn the cakes out to cool. Clean the tins and repeat, making two more sponge layers, colouring one yellow and one green. Turn the cakes out to cool and repeat the process, colouring the last two layers one blue and one purple.

When completely cool, place the purple layer on a cake stand and spread on a thin layer of buttercream. Top with a blue layer, spread another layer of buttercream over and continue spreading and layering with the green, yellow, orange and red cakes. Place a quarter of the remaining buttercream in a piping bag fitted with a star nozzle. Spread the remaining buttercream over the top and round the sides with a palette knife, then smooth round the sides of the cake with a serrated icing smoother. Pipe a shell border round the top and base of the cake and scatter coloured sprinkles over.

Colour 50 g/2 oz batches of sugapaste blue, purple, green and orange. Roll out the colours thinly on a surface dusted with icing sugar and cut out large and small disc shapes with small round cutters. Press the discs round the sides of the cake as shown to finish.

Emerald Tones Cake

Serves 18

For the cake base:

1 x 20 cm/8 inch square chocolate
cake (*see* page 28)

To decorate:

$^1/_2$ batch buttercream (*see* page 40)
1.35 kg/2$^3/_4$ lb ready-to-roll
sugarpaste icing
icing sugar, for dusting
green paste food colouring

Trim the top of the cake flat if it has peaked, cut the cake in half horizontally and spread with a little buttercream, then spread the remainder over the top and sides of the cake.

Cover the cake with 550 g/1$^1/_4$ lb white sugarpaste. Trim round the edges, then place the cake on a 25 cm/10 inch cake board or flat serving plate.

Divide the remaining sugarpaste in half. Keep one half white and colour the other half in three batches of dark, medium and light green. Starting with the dark green paste, roll a small thin strip, 1 cm/$^1/_2$ inches wide x 4 cm/1$^1/_2$ inches long. Roll the strip up in a loose spiral, dampen one end with a little cold boiled water then press onto the side of the cake.

Continue adding the spirals, making a dark double layer all around the base of the cake. Add another double layer of medium green spirals on top for the dark green, then a double light green layer on top of this.

Complete the cake with a layer of white spirals across the top edge and over the top of the cake. Add an emerald green satin ribbon and bow to complete the cake.

Silver Wedding Cake

C

Serves 80–100

For the cake base:

1 x 25 cm/10 inch round rich fuit cake (*see* page 25), covered with almond paste (*see* page 45)
1 x 20 cm/8 inch round rich fruit cake, covered with almond paste
1 x 15 cm/6 inch round rich fruit cake, covered with almond paste

To decorate:

2.25 kg/4¹/₂ lb ready-to-roll sugarpaste icing
icing sugar, for dusting
3 batches royal icing (*see* page 41)
edible silver balls

Divide the sugarpaste into 1 kg/2 lb, 750 g/1¹/₂ lb and 500 g/1 lb 2 oz batches. Cover the largest cake with the largest batch (*see* page 48). Repeat to cover the medium and small cakes.

Place the large cake on a 40 cm/14 inch round cake drum. Place the medium cake on a thin 20 cm/8 inch round board and the small cake on a thin 15 cm/6 inch cake board. Stack the cakes on top of each other using dowelling (*see* page 51).

Place one quarter of the royal icing in a piping bag fitted with a small plain nozzle. Pipe a border of small dots round the base of the large cake, then repeat with the medium and small cakes. Mark the flower shapes as a guide onto the sides of the cake with a small skewer. Fill a bag fitted with a small plain nozzle with royal icing. Pipe the outline of the petals round the guide then take a fine paintbrush and dampen the tip with a little cold boiled water. Use the brush to pull the icing from the outside into the middle of the flower. Place a small silver ball in the centre of each flower. Pipe leaves and squiggles in a random pattern onto the sides of the cake to represent lace work. Stick silver balls onto the cake at intervals. Repeat with the top two tiers and leave the icing to dry out for 5 hours.

Classic Couple Wedding Cake

Serves 80–100

For the cake base:

1 each 15 cm/6 inch, 20 cm/8 inch
and 25 cm/10 inch round rich fruit
cakes, covered in almond paste
(*see* pages 25 and 45)

To decorate:

3 kg/6 lb 10 oz ready-to-roll
sugarpaste
icing sugar, for dusting
$1/2$ batch royal icing
ivory shimmer lustre powder
seed pearl trim
450 g/1 lb flower paste
cornflour, for dusting
black, pink and light brown paste
food colourings
net fabric

Divide the sugarpaste into 1 kg/$2^1/_4$ lb, 700 g/$1^1/_2$ lb and 450 g/1 lb batches, reserving the remainder. Knead each batch until soft, then on a surface dusted with icing sugar roll out to circles large enough to cover the top and sides of each cake. Place the large cake on a 35 cm/14 inch round cake drum, the medium cake on a thin, 20 cm/8 inch round board and the small cake on a thin, 15 cm/6 inch cake board. Brush the almond paste with a little cold boiled water and cover each cake with the sugarpaste circles as per instructions on page 48.

Roll out the remaining sugarpaste thinly and cut out 18 strips 4 cm/$1^1/_2$ inches wide and long enough to go from top to bottom and partway into the centre of each cake as shown. Lightly dab the underside of each strip with royal icing and position at intervals as shown. With a dry pastry brush, lightly flick the ivory dusting powder evenly over the cake. Push four sticks of wooden or plastic dowelling, cut to the depth of the cake, evenly into the large cake base. Repeat with the medium cake. These will take the weight of the cake layers. Stack the cakes on top of each other. Place the pearl trim around the base of each tier.

Roll out a 12 cm/$4^1/_2$ inch circle of flower paste on a surface dusted with cornflour. Flute the edges, then drape over the edge of the top tier for the bride's gown. Model two white bodies. Colour a little paste black, roll into sausages for the groom's legs and feet. Colour a little paste for the skin and model the heads, bride's arms and groom's hands. Colour a little paste brown and model the hair. Secure the heads with toothpicks. Stick all the pieces together with a little royal icing and position on the top tier. Pipe on details with dots of royal icing and paint on the faces. Make a veil with a scrap of net fabric.

Lacework Wedding Cake

Serves 60–70

For the cake base:

1 x 20 cm/8 inch round rich fruit cake
(*see* page 25), covered in almond
paste (*see* page 45)
1 x 15 cm/6 inch round rich fruit cake,
covered in almond paste

To decorate:

1.24 kg/2 lb 4 oz ready-to-roll
sugarpaste icing
peach and pale green paste
food colouring
icing sugar, for dusting
3 batches royal icing (*see* page 41)

Place the large cake on a 30 cm/12 inch round cake drum. Place the small cake on a thin 15 cm/6 inch round board.

Colour 350 g/12 oz sugarpaste peach and 350 g/12 oz pale green. Take balls of peach icing and model into petal shapes then roll around a centre to make roses (*see* page 47). Make 8 peach roses and leave them to harden for 3 hours in empty egg boxes lined with crumpled foil. Repeat with 350 g/12 oz white sugarpaste to make 8 white roses. Roll out the green icing on a surface lightly dusted with icing sugar and stamp out 40 small green leaves and buds. Leave to dry out for 3 hours on nonstick baking parchment.

Coat each cake with royal icing (*see* page 49). Stack the cakes on top of each other, using dowelling (*see* page 51). Fill a piping bag fitted with a medium plain nozzle with royal icing and pipe dots round the base of each cake to make a border. Pipe 'S' shaped swirls and squiggles in a haphazard pattern on the top and sides of the cake as shown.

Mould white sugarpaste trimmings into a pyramid shape and stick the peach and white roses onto this as shown, filling in the gaps with small green leaves and buds. Arrange the remaining roses and leaves on the cake as shown.

.

Tiered Rose Petal Cake

ℰ

Serves 80–100

For the cake base:

1 each 15 cm/6 inch, 20 cm/8 inch
and 25 cm/10 inch round rich fruit
cakes, covered in almond paste
(*see* pages 25 and 45)

To decorate:

2.25 kg/5 lb ready-to-roll sugarpaste
450 g/1 lb flower paste
light and deeper pink
paste food colourings
cornflour, for dusting
1/2 batch royal icing

Divide the sugarpaste into 1 kg/2¹/₄ lb, 700 g/1¹/₂ lb and 450 g/1 lb batches. Knead each batch until soft, then roll out to circles large enough to cover the top and sides of each cake. Place the large cake on a 35 cm/ 14 inch round cake drum. Place the medium cake on a thin, 20 cm/8 inch round board and the small cake on a thin, 15 cm/6 inch cake board. Brush the almond paste with a little cold boiled water, then cover each cake with the appropriate sugarpaste circles as per the instructions on page 48.

Push four sticks of wooden or plastic dowelling, cut to the depth of the cake, evenly into the large cake base. Repeat with the medium cake. These will take the weight of the cake layers. Stack the cakes on top of each other.

Colour three quarters of the flower paste pale pink and one quarter deeper pink. Roll out the pink paste thinly on a surface lightly dusted with cornflour. Cut out 50 large, 50 medium and 50 small petals using petal cutters. Curl the petals and leave to dry in egg boxes lined with crumpled foil until firm. Use the deeper pink paste to make 10 rose centres (*see* page 47) and leave to dry in crumpled foil in egg boxes for 24 hours.

Place a dab of royal icing on each rose petal and arrange around the sides of the cake as shown. Position the deeper pink rose centres as shown, then attach paler pink petals around the centres to build up open roses. Scatter a few petals loosely around the base to finish.

Romantic Roses Cake

Serves 8–12

For the cake base:

1 x 15 cm/6 inch round Madeira cake
(*see* page 29)
3 tbsp apricot glaze

To decorate:

450 g/1 lb ready-to-roll
sugarpaste icing
pink, red and green paste
food colouring
icing sugar, for dusting
225 g/8 oz flower paste
$^1/_2$ batch royal icing (*see* page 41)

Trim the top of the cake flat if it has peaked and brush the glaze over the top and sides of the cake.

Colour the sugarpaste icing pale pink with a few dots of paste food colouring. Roll the icing into a ball and flatten out, then roll out on a surface lightly dusted with icing sugar to a circle large enough to cover the top and sides of the cake. Using both hands, carefully lift the sugarpaste over the cake and smooth down over the top and sides. Trim away the edges then place the cake on a 20 cm/8 inch cake board or flat serving plate.

Colour three quarters of the flower paste red and the rest green. Mould the red flower paste into 3 roses (*see* page 47) then roll out the green icing thinly, cut into leaves and mark on veins with a sharp knife. Leave the roses and leaves for 2–3 hours in egg boxes lined with crumped foil until firm.

Place the royal icing in a piping bag fitted with a small plain nozzle and pipe small dots on the top and sides of the cake. Arrange the roses and leaves on top of the cake, attaching them to the cake with a dab of royal icing. Trim the base of the cake with a strip of thin red satin ribbon and attach with a dab of royal icing.

Pink ❧ Orange Floral Wedding Cake

Serves 90

For the cake base:

1 x 13 cm/5 inch Madeira cake,
covered in almond paste
(*see* pages 29 and 45)
1 x 18 cm/7 inch Madeira cake,
covered in almond paste
1 x 25 cm/10 inch Madeira cake,
covered in almond paste

To decorate:

700 g/1¹/₂ lb flower paste
(*see* page 44)
yellow, dark pink, orange and
green paste food colourings
cornflour, for dusting
6 batches vanilla buttercream
(*see* page 40)
pale lemon paper ribbon

Make the flowers. Colour 125 g/4 oz of the flower paste yellow, then divide the remaining paste into three equal pieces and colour one dark pink, one orange and one green. Dust chrysanthemum flower moulds lightly with a little cornflour. Take a small ball of yellow paste and press into the centre of the mould. Press a circle of dark pink over the yellow ball and push right into the flower mould with your fingertips. Push the flower out onto a sheet of nonstick baking parchment. Repeat with the orange paste. Make seven orange and seven pink flowers. Roll the green paste until soft, press into leaf moulds and press out 30 leaves with a veined pattern. Leave all the flowers and leaves to dry for 24 hours.

Place the small cake on a thin, 15 cm/6 inch square board, the medium cake on a thin 20 cm/8 in board and the large on a 30 cm/12 inch square cake board. Push four sticks of thin wooden or plastic dowelling, cut to the depth of the cake, into the base of the large and medium cakes. Spread the buttercream over the top of each cake and smooth level with an icing rule. Spread the remaining buttercream around the sides with a palette knife and smooth flat with a smoother. Trim the top and side joins, then stack the cakes on top of each other.

Place the paper ribbon around the base of each cake and secure with buttercream. Fill a paper icing bag fitted with a no 3 plain nozzle with buttercream and pipe a lacy design onto the ribbon as shown. Arrange the flowers and leaves on the cake as shown just before serving.

Blue Lacework Cake

🍂

Serves 15–20

For the cake base:

1 x 15 cm/6 inch round rich fruit cake (*see* page 25), covered in almond paste (*see* page 45)

To decorate:

450 g/1 lb ready-to-roll sugarpaste
pale blue paste food colouring
icing sugar, for dusting
1 batch royal icing (*see* page 41)
75 g/3 oz white sugarpaste roses
(*see* page 47)

Colour the sugarpaste pale blue with paste food colouring and use to cover the cake. Trim away the edges.

Place the cake on a 20 cm/8 inch round board and attach a net frill round the base. Place one quarter of the royal icing in a piping bag fitted with a small plain nozzle and pipe a border of small dots round the base of the cake.

Mark star flower shapes as a guide onto the sides of the cake with a small skewer. Fill a piping bag fitted with a small plain nozzle with the remaining royal icing.

Pipe a thin line round the outline of the petals then take a fine paintbrush and dampen the tip with a little cold boiled water. Use the brush to drag the icing from the outside of the outline into the middle of the flower. Pipe a small circlet of dots in the centre of each flower. Repeat, covering the sides of the cake. Pipe swags in small dotted lines on the top edge of the cake

Attach the white roses on top of the cake with a dab of royal icing and leave the icing to dry out for 5 hours.

Sleeping Angel Cake

🍼

Serves 40

For the cake base:

1 x 23 cm/9 inch, square
Madeira cake (see page 29)
1 x 16 cm/6 inch, square
Madeira cake

To decorate:

1 batch vanilla buttercream
(see page 40)
1.8 kg/4 lb ready-to-roll sugarpaste
pink, flesh and brown paste
food colourings
icing sugar, for dusting
2 tbsp royal icing (see page 41)

Trim the tops of the cakes if they have peaked. Cut each cake in half horizontally and spread one half with a little buttercream. Place the other layer on top and spread the remaining buttercream over the top and sides of the cakes.

Colour 1.25 kg/2^1/$_2$ lb sugarpaste light pink. Use 875 g/1^3/$_4$ lb pink sugarpaste to cover the large cake (see page 48), then place on a 30 cm/12 inch cake board. Repeat to cover the small cake with the remaining pink sugarpaste and place on a thin cake board. Place the small cake on top of the larger one.

Colour 50 g/2 oz sugarpaste flesh toned. Roll half into a ball for the angel's head, two sausages for arms and two tiny balls for feet. Roll 50 g/2 oz white sugarpaste into a triangular shape for the body, then position the pieces onto the small cake as shown. Mark a face on the angel with a skewer, then colour the royal icing brown and place in a piping bag fitted with a no 1 straight nozzle. Pipe strands on the head for hair.

Roll the remaining white sugarpaste out thinly and cut into thin strips 2 cm/ ^{3}/$_4$ inch wide. Dampen the underside of each strip with a little cold boiled water and press round the base of the large and small cakes. Make bows with trailing ribbons for each of the cake corners. Re-roll the trimmings and cut out small stars with a star cutter, along with two little wings. Stick the stars onto both the cakes as shown, in a cascade, one on top of the angel's head and the wings on her back.

Daisy Chain Lemon Cupcakes

Makes 12

125 g/4 oz caster sugar
125 g/4 oz soft tub margarine
2 medium eggs
125 g/4 oz self-raising flour
1/2 tsp baking powder
1 tsp lemon juice

To decorate:

50 g/2 oz ready-to-roll
sugarpaste icing
yellow piping icing tube
225 g/8 oz fondant icing sugar
lemon yellow food colouring

Preheat the oven to 190°C/375°F/Gas Mark 5. Line a bun tray with 12 paper cases.

Place all the cupcake ingredients in a large bowl and beat with an electric mixer for about 2 minutes until smooth. Fill the paper cases halfway up with the mixture.

Bake for about 15 minutes until firm, risen and golden. Remove to a wire rack to cool.

Roll out the icing thinly and stamp out small daisies with a fluted daisy cutter. Pipe a small yellow dot of icing into the centre of each and leave to dry out for 1 hour. Blend the fondant icing sugar with a little water and a few dots of yellow colouring to make a thick, easy-to-spread icing, then smooth over the top of each cupcake. Decorate with the cut-out daisies immediately and leave to set for 1 hour. Keep for 3 days in an airtight container.

Ladybird Cake

Serves 20

For the cake base:

1 x 23 cm/9 inch, all-in-one quick-mix sponge (see page 32)
450 g/1 lb apricot glaze (see page 42)
1 x 15 cm/6 inch, round all-in-one quick-mix sponge

To decorate:

1.7 kg/3³/₄ lb ready-to-roll sugarpaste
blue, red, black and green paste food colourings
icing sugar, for dusting
¹/₂ batch vanilla buttercream (see page 40)
confectioner's glaze

Trim the top of the large cake level if it has peaked, then brush half the apricot glaze over the top and sides of the cake. Colour 900 g/2 lb of the sugarpaste pale blue and use to cover the large cake (see page 48). Transfer to a cake board or plate. Trim the smaller cake into a dome shape, then cut a ridge down the centre for the ladybird's body. Brush the remaining apricot glaze over the cake. Colour 400 g/14 oz sugarpaste red and use to cover the smaller cake. Spread the centre of the larger cake with buttercream and lift the smaller cake on top. Reserve a very small amount of the remaining sugarpaste and colour half of the rest black and half green.

Roll out the green sugarpaste and cut out blades of grass with a sharp knife. Dampen and press them around the bottom edge of the larger cake. Shape the ladybird's head from a ball of black sugarpaste. Shape two antennae, stick onto the head with edible glue and leave to set. Shape six legs and brush these and the head and antennae with confectioner's glaze. Cut out about 12 thin circles from black sugarpaste, 1 cm/¹/₂ inch in diameter. Dampen and press over the body. Shape two small pieces of white sugarpaste into circles for eyes, with smaller black pieces for pupils, dampen and press into place. Shape a mouth from a small sausage of white sugarpaste. Colour a tiny amount of white sugarpaste pink using just a dot of red colouring and roll into two balls. Dampen the mouth and press into place with the two small balls of pink sugarpaste at each end. Fix the head and legs in place with a little cold boiled water. Colour the remaining buttercream green, spoon it into a piping bag fitted with a fine plain nozzle and pipe wiggly lines around the base of the ladybird for 'grass' to finish.

Pretty Handbag Cake

Serves 12–16

For the cake base:

1 x 25 cm/10 inch, round
Madeira cake
(see page 29)

To decorate:

200 g/7 oz flower paste
(see page 44)
icing sugar, for dusting
brown and pink paste food colourings
1½ batches vanilla buttercream
(see page 40)
700 g/1½ lb ready-to-roll sugarpaste
¼ batch royal icing (see page 41)
gold lustre powder

Roll out the flower paste on a surface dusted with icing sugar and cut out two 2 x 23 cm/1 x 9 inch strips and four 2.5 x 5 cm/1 x 2 inch strips. Loop the shorter strips in half as shown and secure with a little cold boiled water. Add a tiny ball of white to each for the rivets. Do the same with the ends of the longer strips and then arrange them as shown, hanging over a bottle or rolling pin to dry. With the offcuts, model the tassel, then colour a little light brown to make the zip and tassel top.

Cut the cake in half across the middle and sandwich the halves together with half the buttercream. Stand the cake up on the cut edge and trim all round to make a smooth bag shape. Cover with the rest of the buttercream.

Colour 700 g/1½ lb sugarpaste pink then roll out to a piece large enough to cover the cake. Lift this carefully over the cake and smooth down the top and sides. Press an indentation where the zip will fit. Trim round the base and place on a large plate.

Roll out the remaining white sugarpaste into long sausages to fit all round the base of the cake and two strips over the top. Attach these and the rest of the decorations with dots of royal icing.

Make tiny sausages from the scraps of light brown flower paste and tuck them into the handles to look like links, then paint them with gold lustre powder mixed with a little water to finish.

Cakes for Afternoon Tea

Add a little decadence to your afternoon. Instead of heading over to your local café and picking up a muffin or slice, make a little indulgent treat yourself. You'll be surprised at just how much tastier a Coconut & Lime Muffin or a slice of a homemade Marmalade Loaf Cake is than that blueberry muffin you were going to grab. Pair them with a pot of coffee or tea for an extra special break or fabulous tea party with friends.

Pineapple, Cream Cheese & Carrot Muffins

Makes 12

175 g/6 oz self-raising
wholemeal flour
1 tsp baking powder
$^1/_2$ tsp ground cinnamon
pinch salt
150 ml/$^1/_4$ pint sunflower oil
150 g/5 oz soft light
brown sugar
3 medium eggs, beaten
50 g/2 oz soft dried
pineapple, chopped
225 g/8 oz carrots, peeled and
finely grated

To decorate:

75 g/3 oz cream cheese
175 g/6 oz golden icing sugar
2 tsp lemon juice
50 g/2 oz soft dried pineapple
pieces, thinly sliced

Preheat the oven to 180°C/350°F/Gas Mark 4. Lightly oil a deep 12-hole muffin tray or line with deep paper cases.

Sift the flour, baking powder, cinnamon and salt into a bowl, including any bran from the sieve. Add the oil, sugar, eggs, chopped pineapple and grated carrots.

Beat until smooth, then spoon into the muffin cases. Bake for 20–25 minutes until risen and golden. Cool on a wire rack.

To decorate the muffins, beat the cream cheese and icing sugar together with the lemon juice to make a spreading consistency. Swirl the icing over the top of each cupcake, then top with a piece of dried pineapple. If chilled and sealed in an airtight container, these will keep for 3–4 days.

Blue Daisy Cupcakes

Makes 12

For the cakes:

1 batch vanilla cupcakes
(*see* page 31)
3 tbsp apricot glaze

To decorate:

700 g/1 1/2 lb ready-to-roll
sugarpaste
blue and yellow paste food
colourings
icing sugar, for dusting
1/4 batch royal icing
tiny gold and silver seed sprinkles

Colour 125 g/4 oz of the sugarpaste blue, cover in clingfilm and reserve. Trim the cupcakes to give them a flat top and brush the apricot glaze over.

Roll out the white sugarpaste thinly on a surface lightly dusted with icing sugar. Using a round cutter, stamp out 12 circles 6 cm/2 1/2 inches wide, then press down with an embossing tool to make a raised pattern in the icing. Stick the discs onto the tops of the cakes.

Gather up the white scraps and roll out thinly. Stamp out 12 large star flowers, 12 medium star flowers, 24 small star flowers and 24 small blossom flowers with cutters. Place the medium star flowers in the large star flower shapes. Shape the flowers to curve the petals with a small bone tool.

Roll out the blue sugarpaste on a small board or surface lightly dusted with icing sugar. Stamp put 80 large blossom flowers, 80 medium and 80 small blossom flowers with blossom cutters. Colour the royal icing a pale yellow and place in a paper icing bag fitted with a no 0 plain nozzle. Pipe small dots into the centres of the blue flowers.

Attach the flowers around the outer edge of each cake with a dot of royal icing. Arrange the gold and silver seeds in the centres of the white flowers, then arrange on top of the cake as shown.

Rich Chocolate Cupcakes

Makes 12

175 g/6 oz self-raising flour
25 g/1 oz cocoa powder
175 g/6 oz soft light brown sugar
75 g/3 oz butter, melted
2 medium eggs, lightly beaten
1 tsp vanilla extract
40 g/1½ oz maraschino cherries,
drained and chopped

For the chocolate icing:

50 g/2 oz dark chocolate
25 g/1 oz unsalted butter
25 g/1 oz icing sugar, sifted

For the cherry icing:

125 g/4 oz icing sugar
7 g/¼ oz unsalted butter, melted
1 tsp syrup from the
maraschino cherries
3 maraschino cherries, halved,
to decorate

Preheat the oven to 180°C/350°F/Gas Mark 4, 10 minutes before baking. Line a 12-hole muffin tin or deep bun tray with paper muffin cases. Sift the flour and cocoa powder into a bowl. Stir in the sugar, then add the melted butter, eggs and vanilla extract. Beat together with a wooden spoon for 3 minutes, or until well blended.

Divide half the mixture between six of the paper cases. Dry the cherries thoroughly on absorbent kitchen paper, then fold into the remaining mixture and spoon into the rest of the paper cases.

Bake on the shelf above the centre of the preheated oven for 20 minutes, or until a skewer inserted into the centre of a cake comes out clean. Transfer to a wire rack and leave to cool.

For the chocolate icing, melt the chocolate and butter in a heatproof bowl set over a saucepan of simmering water. Remove from the heat and leave to cool for 3 minutes, stirring occasionally. Stir in the icing sugar. Spoon over the six plain chocolate cakes and leave to set.

For the cherry icing, sift the icing sugar into a bowl and stir in 1 tablespoon boiling water, the butter and cherry syrup. Spoon the icing over the remaining six cakes, decorate each with a halved cherry and leave to set.

Afternoon Tea Cake

Serves 40

For the cake base:

1 x 20 cm/8 inch round Madeira
cake (*see* page 29), covered in
almond paste (*see* page 45)
1 x 15 cm/6 inch round Madeira
cake, covered in almond paste

To decorate:

1.75 kg/3^1/$_2$ lb ready-to-roll
sugarpaste icing
icing sugar, for dusting
pink, blue, yellow and green paste
food colouring
^{1}/$_2$ batch royal icing (*see* page 41)
edible silver balls

Cut off 450 g/1 lb sugarpaste and set aside. Divide the
remaining sugarpaste into 550 g/1^1/$_4$ lb and 500 g/1 lb 2 oz
batches. Cover the larger cake with the large sugarpaste
batch (*see* page 48). Trim the edges then repeat to cover the
smaller cake.

Place the large cake on a 30 cm/12 inch cake drum and the
smaller one on a 15 cm/6 inch thin round cake board. Stack
the cakes using dowelling (*see* page 51).

Colour the remaining sugarpaste in small batches of light and
dark pink, blue, yellow and green. Model open roses with the
coloured sugarpaste (*see* page 47) and place in empty egg
boxes lined with crumpled foil. Cut out small green leaves and
mark on veins with a sharp knife. Leave the roses and leaves
to harden for 4 hours.

Colour the royal icing pale pink and pipe a shell border round
the base of each cake. Position the flowers on top and round
the side of the cake and place the leaves under the flowers.
Stick the flowers in place with a dab of royal icing then press
the silver balls on top of each cake to finish.

Moist Mocha ❧ Coconut Cake

Makes 9 squares

3 tbsp ground coffee
5 tbsp hot milk
75 g/3 oz butter
175 g/6 oz golden syrup
25 g/1 oz soft light brown sugar
40 g/1¹/₂ oz desiccated coconut
150 g/5 oz plain flour
25 g/1 oz cocoa powder
¹/₂ tsp bicarbonate of soda
2 medium eggs, lightly beaten
3 chocolate flakes, to decorate

For the coffee icing:

225 g/8 oz icing sugar, sifted
125 g/4 oz butter, softened

Preheat the oven to 170°C/325°F/Gas Mark 3, 10 minutes before baking. Lightly oil and line a deep 20.5 cm/8 inch square tin with nonstick baking parchment. Place the ground coffee in a small bowl and pour over the hot milk. Leave to infuse for 5 minutes, then strain through a tea strainer or a sieve lined with muslin. You will end up with about 4 tablespoons of liquid. Reserve.

Put the butter, golden syrup, sugar and coconut in a small heavy-based saucepan and heat gently until the butter has melted and the sugar dissolved. Sift the flour, cocoa powder and bicarbonate of soda together and stir into the melted mixture with the eggs and 3 tablespoons of the coffee-infused milk.

Pour the mixture into the prepared tin. Bake on the centre shelf of the preheated oven for 45 minutes, or until the cake is well risen and firm to the touch. Leave in the tin for 10 minutes to cool slightly, then turn out onto a wire rack to cool completely.

For the icing, gradually add the icing sugar to the softened butter and beat together until mixed. Add the remaining 1 tablespoon of the coffee-infused milk and beat until light and fluffy.

Carefully spread the coffee icing over the top of the cake, then cut into 9 squares. Decorate each square with a small piece of chocolate flake and serve.

Butterfly Trio Cupcakes

Makes 12

For the cakes:

1 batch vanilla cupcakes
(*see* page 31)

To decorate:

1 batch vanilla buttercream
(*see* page 40)
350 g/12 oz ready-to-roll sugarpaste
cream and pink paste
food colourings
icing sugar, for dusting
gold lustre powder
edible gold star sprinkles

Trim the top of each cake flat if they have peaked slightly. Place the buttercream in a large piping bag fitted with a star nozzle. Colour half the sugarpaste pale cream, one quarter dark pink and one quarter pale pink.

Roll the cream sugarpaste out thinly on a surface lightly dusted with icing sugar and cut out 12 large butterflies with a cutter, or with a sharp knife following your own design. Press a pattern onto the wings with an embossing tool, or mark on with a skewer. Repeat using the deep pink sugarpaste to make 12 medium-size butterflies and the pale pink sugarpaste to make 12 smaller ones. Tilt the wings upwards and leave to dry between two open folded sheets of nonstick baking parchment for 2 hours to firm.

Dust the cream butterflies with a little gold powder, applied with a dry paintbrush.

Pipe the buttercream onto the cakes in large swirls, then scatter with the gold star sprinkles. Arrange a large, medium and small butterfly on each cake to serve.

Double Cherry Cupcakes

Makes 12 large cupcakes or 18 fairy cakes

50 g/2 oz glacé cherries, washed, dried and chopped
125 g/4 oz self-raising flour
25 g/1 oz dried morello cherries
125 g/4 oz soft margarine
125 g/4 oz caster sugar
2 medium eggs
$^1/_2$ tsp almond extract

To decorate:

125 g/4 oz fondant icing sugar
pale pink liquid food colouring
40 g/1$^1/_2$ oz glacé cherries

Preheat the oven to 190°C/375°F/Gas Mark 5. Line a 12-hole muffin tray with deep paper cases, or two trays with 18 fairy-cake cases.

Dust the chopped glacé cherries lightly in a tablespoon of the flour, then mix with the morello cherries and set aside. Sift the rest of the flour into a bowl, then add the margarine, sugar, eggs and almond extract. Beat for about 2 minutes until smooth, then fold in the cherries.

Spoon the batter into the paper cases and bake for 15–20 minutes until well risen and springy in the centre. Turn out to cool on a wire rack.

To decorate the cupcakes, trim the tops level. Mix the icing sugar with 2–3 teaspoon warm water and a few drops of pink food colouring to make a thick consistency. Spoon the icing over each cupcake filling right up to the edge. Chop the cherries finely and sprinkle over the icing. Leave to set for 30 minutes. Keep for 3 days in an airtight container.

Toffee Walnut Swiss Roll

Serves 10–12

4 large eggs, separated
1/2 tsp cream of tartar
125 g/4 oz icing sugar,
plus extra for dusting
1/2 tsp vanilla extract
125 g/4 oz self-raising flour

For the toffee walnut filling:

2 tbsp plain flour
150 ml/1/4 pint milk
5 tbsp golden syrup or maple syrup
2 large egg yolks, beaten
100 g/31/2 oz walnuts or pecans,
toasted and chopped
300 ml/1/2 pint double
cream, whipped

Preheat the oven to 190°C/375°F/Gas Mark 5, 10 minutes before baking. Lightly oil and line a Swiss roll tin with nonstick baking parchment. Beat the egg whites and cream of tartar until softly peaking. Gradually beat in 50 g/2 oz of the icing sugar until stiff peaks form. In another bowl, beat the egg yolks with the remaining icing sugar until thick. Beat in the vanilla extract. Gently fold in the flour and egg whites alternately using a metal spoon or rubber spatula. Do not overmix. Spoon into the tin and spread evenly. Bake in the oven for 12 minutes, or until well risen, golden and the cake springs back when pressed with a clean finger. Lay a clean tea towel on a work surface, lay a piece of baking parchment about 33 cm/13 inches long on it and dust with icing sugar. As soon as the cake is cooked, turn out onto the paper. Peel off the lining paper and cut off the crisp edges of the cake. Starting at one narrow end, roll the cake with the paper and towel. Transfer to a wire rack and cool completely.

For the filling, put the flour, milk and syrup into a small saucepan and place over a gentle heat. Bring to the boil, whisking until thick and smooth. Remove from the heat and slowly beat into the beaten egg yolks. Pour back into the saucepan and cook over a low heat until it thickens and coats the back of a spoon. Strain into a bowl and stir in the chopped nuts. Cool, stirring occasionally, then fold in about half of the whipped cream. Unroll the cooled cake and spread the filling over it. Re-roll and decorate with the remaining cream. Sprinkle with the icing sugar and serve.

Coconut & Lime Muffins

Makes 12

125 g/4 oz soft margarine
125 g/4 oz golden caster sugar
2 medium eggs
50 g/2 oz desiccated coconut
1 lime
125 g/4 oz self-raising flour
1 tsp baking powder
2 tbsp milk

To decorate:

40 g/1½ oz unsalted butter
125 g/4 oz icing sugar
50 g/2 oz coconut chips
zest of 1 lime, grated

Preheat the oven to 180°C/350°F/Gas Mark 4. Line a deep 12-hole muffin tray with deep paper cases.

Place the margarine and caster sugar in a bowl and add the eggs and coconut. Finely grate the zest from the lime into the bowl, then squeeze in the juice. Sift in the flour and baking powder.

Add the milk and whisk together for about 2 minutes with an electric beater, or by hand until smooth, then spoon into the paper cases. Bake for 15–20 minutes until golden and firm. Cool on a wire rack.

To decorate the muffins, beat the butter and icing sugar together until smooth, then pipe or swirl onto each muffin. Press the coconut chips into the buttercream and then scatter the grated lime zest on top. Keep for 3 days in an airtight container in a cool place.

Pink ❧ Blue Flower Cupcakes

Makes 12

For the cakes:

1 batch vanilla cupcakes
(*see* page 31)
2 tbsp apricot glaze
(*see* page 42)

To decorate:

450 g/1 lb ready-to-roll sugarpaste
pink and pale turquoise paste
food colourings
icing sugar, for dusting
125 g/4 oz flower paste
(*see* page 44)
cornflour, for dusting
edible seed pearl decorations
light pink and magenta
dusting powders

Trim the cupcakes to give them a flat surface and brush the apricot glaze over.

Colour the sugarpaste pale turquoise, then roll out thinly on a surface lightly dusted with icing sugar. Using a fluted cutter, stamp out 12 circles, 6 cm/2^1/$_2$ inches wide. Stick the discs onto the cakes and smooth out lightly with your fingertips. Take a quilting tool and mark lines across in two directions to make diamond shapes. Decorate six cakes with a quilted pattern and leave six plain.

Colour the flower paste pink and roll out very thinly on a small board dusted with cornflour. Using a daisy cutter, cut out four daisies, curl up the edges with a balling tool and press a seed pearl in the centre of each flower. Repeat making four flowers with an open flower cutter and 4 with a four-petal flower cutter. Dust the edges of the petals of the open flower with magenta dusting powder and lightly brush the others with light pink dusting powder. Leave to dry out on a sheet of nonstick baking parchment for 1 hour.

To finish, place the open flowers on the quilted patterned cakes and the other eight on the plain cakes. Dampen the centre of each cake lightly with a cold little boiled water, then press the flower in place.

Chocolate Madeleines

Makes 10

125 g/4 oz butter
125 g/4 oz soft light brown sugar
2 medium eggs, lightly beaten
1 drop almond extract
1 tbsp ground almonds
75 g/3 oz self-raising flour
20 g/³/₄ oz cocoa powder
1 tsp baking powder

To decorate:

5 tbsp apricot conserve
1 tbsp amaretto liqueur,
brandy or orange juice
50 g/2 oz desiccated coconut
10 large chocolate buttons (optional)

Preheat the oven to 180°C/350°F/Gas Mark 4, 10 minutes before baking. Lightly oil 10 dariole moulds and line the bases of each with a small circle of nonstick baking parchment. Stand the moulds on a baking tray. Cream the butter and sugar together until light and fluffy. Gradually add the eggs, beating well between each addition. Beat in the almond extract and ground almonds.

Sift the flour, cocoa powder and baking powder over the creamed mixture. Gently fold in using a metal spoon. Divide the mixture equally between the prepared moulds; each should be about half full.

Bake on the centre shelf of the preheated oven for 20 minutes, or until well risen and firm to the touch. Leave in the tins for a few minutes, then run a small palette knife round the edge and turn out onto a wire rack to cool. Remove the paper circles from the sponges.

Heat the conserve with the liqueur, brandy or juice in a small saucepan. Sieve to remove any lumps. If necessary, trim the sponge bases so they are flat. Brush the tops and sides with warm conserve, then roll in the coconut. Top each with a chocolate button, fixed by brushing its base with conserve.

Tropical Mango Muffins

Makes 10

50 g/2 oz soft dried pineapple chunks
50 g/2 oz soft dried papaya pieces
25 g/1 oz soft dried mango pieces
225 g/8 oz plain flour
1 tsp baking powder
1/2 tsp bicarbonate of soda
75 g/3 oz golden caster sugar
1 medium egg
275 ml/9 fl oz milk
zest and 1 tbsp juice from
1 small orange
50 g/2 oz butter, melted and cooled

Preheat the oven to 200°C/400°F/Gas Mark 6. Line a deep muffin tray with 10 deep paper muffin cases. Wet a sharp knife and chop the fruits into small chunks. Set them aside.

Sift the flour, baking powder and bicarbonate of soda into a large bowl. Add the sugar and make a well in the centre. In another bowl, beat the egg and milk together with the orange juice.

Add the milk to the bowl with the melted butter and the orange zest and beat with a fork until all the flour is combined but the mixture is still slightly lumpy. Fold in three-quarters of the chopped fruit and spoon into the paper cases. Sprinkle the remaining fruit over the top of each muffin.

Bake for about 20 minutes until risen, golden and firm. Cool on a wire rack and eat warm or cold. Keep for 24 hours sealed in an airtight container.

Lemony Coconut Cake

Serves 10–12

275 g/10 oz plain flour
2 tbsp cornflour
1 tbsp baking powder
1 tsp salt
150 g/5 oz white vegetable
fat or soft margarine
275 g/10 oz caster sugar
grated zest of 2 lemons
1 tsp vanilla extract
3 large eggs
150 ml/$^{1}/_{4}$ pint milk
4 tbsp Malibu or rum
450 g/1 lb jar lemon curd
lime zest, to decorate

For the frosting:

275 g/10 oz caster sugar
125 ml/4 fl oz water
1 tbsp glucose
$^{1}/_{4}$ tsp salt
1 tsp vanilla extract
3 large egg whites
75 g/3 oz desiccated coconut

Preheat the oven to 180°C/350°F/Gas Mark 4, 10 minutes before baking. Lightly oil and flour two 20.5 cm/8 inch nonstick cake tins. Sift the flour, cornflour, baking powder and salt into a large bowl and add the white vegetable fat or margarine, sugar, lemon zest, vanilla extract, eggs and milk. With an electric whisk on a low speed, beat until blended, adding a little extra milk if the mixture is very stiff. Increase the speed to medium and beat for about 2 minutes.

Divide the mixture between the tins and smooth the tops evenly. Bake in the oven for 20–25 minutes until the cakes feel firm and are cooked. Remove from the oven and cool before removing from the tins.

Put all the frosting ingredients, except the coconut, into a heatproof bowl placed over a saucepan of simmering water. Using an electric whisk, blend the frosting ingredients on a low speed. Increase the speed to high and beat for 7 minutes until the whites are stiff and glossy. Remove the bowl from the heat and continue beating until cool. Cover with clingfilm.

Using a serrated knife, split the cake layers horizontally in half and sprinkle each cut surface with the Malibu or rum. Sandwich the cakes together with the lemon curd and press lightly. Spread the top and sides generously with the frosting, swirling and peaking the top. Sprinkle the coconut over the top of the cake and gently press onto the sides to cover. Decorate with the lime zest. Serve.

Butterscotch Loaf

Serves 8

1 banana, peeled, weighing
about 100 g/3^1/$_2$ oz
125 g/4 oz soft margarine
125 g/4 oz golden caster sugar
2 medium eggs
1 tsp almond extract
^{1}/$_2$ tsp vanilla extract
125 g/4 oz self-raising flour
75 g/3 oz dark chocolate chips
75 g/3 oz walnuts, chopped

To decorate:

50 g/2 oz natural icing sugar
25 g/1 oz golden lump sugar,
chopped

Preheat the oven to 170˚C/325˚F/Gas Mark 3. Grease and line the base of a 1 kg/2 lb loaf tin with a long thin strip of nonstick baking parchment.

Place the banana in a bowl and mash. Add the margarine, sugar and eggs along with the extracts and sift in the flour. Beat until smooth, then stir in the chocolate chips and add half the chopped walnuts. Stir until smooth, then spoon into the tin and spread level.

Bake for about 45 minutes until a skewer inserted into the centre comes out clean. Leave in the tin for 5 minutes, then turn out onto a wire rack, peel away the paper and leave to cool.

To decorate, add 2 teaspoons water to the icing sugar and make into a runny consistency. Drizzle over the cake and sprinkle over the remaining walnuts and the sugar lumps. Leave to set for 30 minutes, then serve sliced.

Petit Fours Hearts

Makes 24 small cakes

For the cake base:

175 g/6 oz butter, softened
175 g/6 oz caster sugar
3 medium eggs, beaten
$^1/_2$ tsp almond extract
150 g/5 oz self-raising flour
25 g/1 oz ground almonds

To decorate:

8 tbsp sieved apricot jam, warmed
225 g/8 oz white marzipan
icing sugar, for dusting
450 g/1 lb each of white, pale pink
and deep rose pink ready-to-roll
sugarpaste icing
edible sugar pearls

Preheat the oven to 180°C/350°F/Gas Mark 4. Grease and line a 23 x 33 cm/ 9 x 13 inch Swiss roll tin. Beat the butter and sugar together until light and fluffy, then gradually beat in the eggs and extract. Fold in the flour and ground almonds with 1 tablespoon cold water until smooth. Spoon into the tin, spreading evenly into the corners. Bake for 20 minutes until firm and golden. Turn out onto a wire rack to cool and peel away the lining paper.

Brush half the apricot jam over the top of the cake. Dust a clean work surface with icing sugar and roll out the marzipan to the same size as the top of the cake. Carefully lift the marzipan onto the top of the cake and smooth flat. Cut the cake into 24 hearts using a heart cutter measuring 5 cm/2 inches across the widest part. Brush the sides of the cakes with the remaining apricot jam.

Roll out 350 g/12 oz of white sugarpaste on a surface lightly dusted with icing sugar and cut into eight squares. Place a white square onto eight of the heart cakes and smooth over to cover the top and sides. Trim the edges and smooth round the base to neaten. Repeat and cover eight cakes with the pale pink and eight with the deep pink sugarpastes. Roll out the remaining white sugarpaste and, using special cutters, cut out four star-flower shapes and four daisy shapes. Pinch the star-flower petals together and make a round shape in each of the daisy petals with a boning tool. Roll tiny pink balls and press into the centre of each flower. Repeat, making eight more flowers with the pale pink and eight more with the deep pink sugarpastes, using edible pearls for the centre of each flower. Brush the underside of each flower with a little cold boiled water and press each one onto a heart cake in a contrasting colour.

Blackcurrant & Lemon Muffins

Makes 12

1 lemon
275 g/10 oz plain flour
1 tbsp baking powder
125 g/4 oz caster sugar
2 medium eggs
275 ml/9 fl oz milk
$1/2$ tsp vanilla extract
75 g/3 oz butter, melted and cooled
150 g/5 oz fresh or frozen
blackcurrants, trimmed

Preheat the oven to 200°C/400°F/Gas Mark 6. Grease or line a deep 12-hole muffin tray with deep paper cases.

Finely grate the zest from the lemon into a bowl, then sift in the flour and baking powder and stir in the sugar. In another bowl, beat the eggs with the milk and vanilla extract.

Make a well in the centre and pour in the egg mixture and the cooled melted butter. Stir together with a fork until just combined and then gently fold in the blackcurrants.

Spoon into the muffin trays and bake for 20 minutes or until firm and golden. Leave in the tins for 4 minutes, then turn out onto a wire rack to finish cooling. Serve warm or cold. Best eaten on the day of baking.

Chocolate Pecan Traybake

Makes 12

175 g/6 oz butter
75 g/3 oz icing sugar, sifted
175 g/6 oz plain flour
25 g/1 oz self-raising flour
25 g/1 oz cocoa powder

For the pecan topping:

75 g/3 oz butter
50 g/2 oz light muscovado sugar
2 tbsp golden syrup
2 tbsp milk
1 tsp vanilla extract
2 medium eggs, lightly beaten
125 g/4 oz pecan halves

Preheat the oven to 180°C/350°F/Gas Mark 4, 10 minutes before baking. Lightly oil and line a 28 x 18 x 2.5 cm/11 x 7 x 1 inch cake tin with nonstick baking parchment. Beat the butter and sugar together until light and fluffy. Sift in the flours and cocoa powder and mix together to form a soft dough.

Press the mixture evenly over the base of the prepared tin. Prick all over with a fork, then bake on the shelf above the centre of the preheated oven for 15 minutes.

Put the butter, sugar, golden syrup, milk and vanilla extract in a small saucepan and heat gently until melted. Remove from the heat and leave to cool for a few minutes, then stir in the eggs and pour over the base. Sprinkle with the nuts.

Bake in the preheated oven for 25 minutes, or until dark golden brown, but still slightly soft. Leave to cool in the tin. When cool, carefully remove from the tin, then cut into 12 squares and serve. Store in an airtight container.

Pretty Pink Cupcakes

č

Makes 12

For the cakes:

1 batch vanilla cupcakes
(*see* page 31)
2 tbsp apricot glaze

To decorate:

700 g/1½ lb ready-to-roll sugarpaste
pink paste food colouring
icing sugar, for dusting
pink lustre powder
1 small tube or 1 tbsp royal icing
(*see* page 41)

Colour half the sugarpaste pink and leave the remainder white. Roll out a small amount of pink and white sugarpaste on a surface dusted with icing sugar and cut out six small pink daisies and six white daisies with a small daisy stamp. Make a pink centre for each one and leave to dry in empty egg boxes lined with crumpled foil. When dry, dust the centre of each one with a little pink lustre powder.

Trim the cupcakes to give them a rounded shape and brush the apricot glaze over. Roll out the remaining pink sugarpaste thinly on a board or surface dusted with icing sugar. Using a round cutter, stamp out six circles 6 cm/2½ inches wide.

Dust the inside of an embossing pattern mould lightly with icing sugar and flick away the excess with a soft paintbrush. Press a circle of sugarpaste into the mould, pressing around the pattern, then lift it out carefully and drape the paste over a cupcake. Press in position, being careful not to touch the design. Repeat with the rest of the pink sugarpaste and five cupcakes. Using the white sugarpaste, repeat with the remaining six cakes. To finish, stick the daisies in position with a small dab of royal icing.

Fruity Buttermilk Muffins

Makes 12

175 g/6 oz self-raising flour
50 g/2 oz wholemeal self-raising flour
1 tsp mixed ground spice
$^{1}/_{2}$ tsp bicarbonate of soda
1 medium egg
2 tbsp fine-cut orange
shred marmalade
125 ml/4 fl oz milk
50 ml/2 fl oz buttermilk
5 tbsp sunflower oil
125 g/4 oz eating apple, peeled,
cored and diced
125 g/4 oz ready-to-eat pitted
prunes, roughly chopped

Preheat the oven to 200°C/400°F/Gas Mark 6. Line a deep 12-hole muffin tray with deep paper cases.

Sift the flours, spice and bicarbonate of soda into a bowl. In another bowl, beat the egg with the marmalade, milk, buttermilk and oil and pour into the dry ingredients.

Stir with a fork until just combined, then fold in the apple and chopped prunes. Spoon into the cases and bake for about 20 minutes until golden, risen and firm to the touch.

Leave in the tins for 4 minutes, then turn out onto a wire rack to finish cooling. Serve warm or cold and eat on the day of baking.

Chocolate Brazil & Polenta Squares

Makes 9 squares

150 g/5 oz shelled Brazil nuts
150 g/5 oz butter, softened
150 g/5 oz soft light brown sugar
2 medium eggs, lightly beaten
75 g/3 oz plain flour
25 g/1 oz cocoa powder
$1/4$ tsp ground cinnamon
1 tsp baking powder
pinch salt
5 tbsp milk
65 g/$2^1/2$ oz instant polenta

Preheat the oven to 180°C/350°F/Gas Mark 4, 10 minutes before baking. Oil and line a deep 18 cm/7 inch square tin with nonstick baking parchment. Finely chop 50 g/2 oz of the Brazil nuts and reserve. Roughly chop the remainder. Cream the butter and sugar together until light and fluffy. Gradually add the eggs, beating well after each addition.

Sift the flour, cocoa powder, cinnamon, baking powder and salt into the creamed mixture and gently fold in using a large metal spoon or spatula. Add the milk, polenta and the roughly chopped Brazil nuts. Fold into the mixture.

Turn the mixture into the prepared tin, levelling the surface with the back of the spoon. Sprinkle the reserved finely chopped Brazil nuts over the top. Bake the cake on the centre shelf of the preheated oven for 45–50 minutes until well risen and lightly browned and when a clean skewer inserted into the centre of the cake for a few seconds comes out clean.

Leave the cake in the tin for 10 minutes to cool slightly, then turn out onto a wire rack and leave to cool completely. Cut the cake into nine equal squares and serve. Store in an airtight container.

Date, Orange & Walnut Muffins

Makes 12

275 g/10 oz plain flour
1 tbsp baking powder
125 g/4 oz golden caster sugar
175 g/6 oz stoned dates, chopped
50 g/2 oz chopped walnuts
1 medium egg
200 ml/7 fl oz milk
finely grated zest and juice of
1 orange
6 tbsp sunflower oil

Preheat the oven to 200°C/400°F/Gas Mark 6. Line a deep 12-hole muffin tray with deep paper cases.

Sift the flour and baking powder into a bowl and make a well in the centre.

Add all the remaining ingredients and beat together until just combined. Spoon the batter into the paper cases and bake for about 16–18 minutes until well risen and firm to the touch.

Serve warm or cold and eat the muffins on the day of baking.

Teatime Cake Pops

Makes 12

For the cakes:

65 g/2^1/$_2$ oz soft-tub margarine or
softened butter
65 g/2^1/$_2$ oz caster sugar
65 g/2^1/$_2$ oz self-raising flour
1 egg
^{1}/$_2$ tsp milk
^{1}/$_2$ tsp vanilla extract

To decorate:

700 g/1^1/$_2$ lb ready-to-roll
sugarpaste
blue and yellow paste food
colourings
^{1}/$_2$ batch vanilla buttercream
(see page 40)
12 thin lollipop sticks
block floristry foam
small seed pearl decorations
^{1}/$_4$ batch royal icing

Preheat the oven to 180°C/350°F/Gas Mark 4. Brush a 12-hole cake pop mould with melted butter. Beat all the ingredients together for 2 minutes until smooth. Spoon 1 heaped teaspoon into each mould. Clamp on the lid and bake for 12 minutes. Test by inserting a cocktail stick into the hole in the moulds – it should come out clean. Turn out to cool on a wire rack.

Colour 125 g/4 oz of the sugarpaste yellow. Colour the rest blue and divide into 12. Roll four blue sugarpaste balls out to circles large enough to cover the cake pops. Coat four cakes thickly in buttercream, drape the sugarpaste over, trim and press the joins together until smooth. Press short, thick sausages of blue sugarpaste onto one sides and shape into the spouts, smoothing to join. Make balls, flatten out and stick in place on top with a little cold boiled water for the lids. Add tiny balls for the handles. Curve small, thin sausages to make the handles and stick in place. Place the teapots on the lollipop sticks upright in the floristry foam.

Make the teacups: trim eight cake pops to make cup shapes. Coat thickly in buttercream, cover with strips and circles of rolled blue sugarpaste, trim and press the joins together until smooth. Model small sausages of blue icing to make the handles, curve round and stick in place. Make small rounds for the saucers and stick in place. Place the teacups on the lollipop sticks and place them in the floristry foam.

Roll out the yellow icing thinly, stamp out small and medium blossom shapes and stick onto the teapots and cups. Decorate the flowers, sides and lids with seed pearls as shown, sticking with small dabs of royal icing.

Chocolate Orange Fudge Cake

Serves 8–10

65 g/2$^{1}/_{2}$ oz cocoa powder
grated zest of 1 orange
350 g/12 oz self-raising flour
2 tsp baking powder
1 tsp bicarbonate of soda
$^{1}/_{2}$ tsp salt
225 g/8 oz light soft brown sugar
175 g/6 oz butter, softened
3 medium eggs
1 tsp vanilla extract
250 ml/9 fl oz sour cream
6 tbsp butter
6 tbsp milk
thinly pared rind of 1 orange
6 tbsp cocoa powder
250 g/9 oz icing sugar, sifted

Preheat the oven to 180˚C/350˚F/Gas Mark 4, 10 minutes before baking. Lightly oil and line two 23 cm/9 inch round cake tins with nonstick baking parchment. Blend the cocoa powder and 50 ml/2 fl oz boiling water until smooth. Stir in the orange zest and reserve. Sift together the flour, baking powder, bicarbonate of soda and salt, then reserve. Cream together the sugar and softened butter and beat in the eggs, one at a time, then the cocoa mixture and vanilla extract. Finally, stir in the flour mixture and the sour cream in alternate spoonfuls.

Divide the mixture between the prepared tins and bake in the preheated oven for 35 minutes, or until the edges of the cake pull away from the tin and the tops spring back when lightly pressed. Cool in the tins for 10 minutes, then turn out onto wire racks to cool.

Gently heat together the butter and milk with the pared orange rind. Simmer for 10 minutes, stirring occasionally. Remove from the heat and discard the orange rind.

Pour the warm orange and milk mixture into a large bowl and stir in the cocoa powder. Gradually beat in the sifted icing sugar and beat until the icing is smooth and spreadable. Place one cake onto a large serving plate. Top with about one quarter of the icing, place the second cake on top, then cover the cake completely with the remaining icing. Serve.

Streusel-Topped Banana Muffins

Makes 6

To decorate:

25 g/1 oz self-raising flour
15 g/¹/₂ oz butter
40 g/1¹/₂ oz demerara sugar
¹/₂ tsp ground cinnamon

To make the muffins:

125 g/4 oz self-raising
wholemeal flour
25 g/1 oz plain flour
2 medium ripe bananas,
about 175 g/6 oz
1 large egg
50 ml/2 fl oz sunflower oil
50 ml/2 fl oz milk

Preheat the oven to 200°C/400°F/Gas Mark 6. Line a deep muffin tray with 6 deep paper cases. Make the topping first by rubbing the butter into the flour until it resembles fine crumbs. Stir in the sugar and cinnamon and set aside.

To make the muffins, sift the flours into a bowl, then make a well in the centre. Mash the bananas with a fork and add them to the bowl.

In another bowl, beat the egg, oil and milk together and then add them to the bowl. Mix together until evenly blended, then spoon into the muffin cases, filling them two-thirds full.

Sprinkle the streusel topping over each muffin and bake for about 25 minutes until golden and a skewer inserted into the centre comes out clean. Eat fresh on the day of baking.

Chocolate Walnut Squares

Makes 24

125 g/4 oz butter
150 g/5 oz dark chocolate,
broken into squares
450 g/1 lb caster sugar
1/2 tsp vanilla extract
200 g/7 oz plain flour
75 g/3 oz self-raising flour
50 g/2 oz cocoa powder
225 g/8 oz mayonnaise, at
room temperature

For the chocolate glaze:

125 g/4 oz dark chocolate,
broken into squares
40 g/1 1/2 oz unsalted butter
24 walnut halves
1 tbsp icing sugar, for dusting

Preheat the oven to 170°C/325°F/Gas Mark 3, 10 minutes before baking. Oil and line a 28 x 18 x 5 cm/11 x 7 x 2 inch cake tin with nonstick baking parchment. Place the butter, chocolate, sugar, vanilla extract and 225 ml/8 fl oz cold water in a heavy-based saucepan. Heat gently, stirring occasionally, until the chocolate and butter have melted, but do not allow to boil.

Sift the flours and cocoa powder into a large bowl and make a well in the centre. Add the mayonnaise and about one third of the chocolate mixture and beat until smooth. Gradually beat in the remaining chocolate mixture. Pour into the tin and bake on the centre shelf of the oven for 1 hour, or until slightly risen and firm to the touch. Place the tin on a wire rack and leave to cool. Remove the cake and peel off the baking parchment.

For the chocolate glaze, place the chocolate and butter in a small saucepan with 1 tablespoon water and heat very gently, stirring occasionally, until melted and smooth. Leave to cool until the chocolate has thickened, then spread evenly over the cake. Chill the cake in the refrigerator for about 5 minutes, then mark into 24 squares.

Lightly dust the walnut halves with a little icing sugar and place one on the top of each square. Cut into pieces and store in an airtight container until ready to serve.

Pistachio Muffins

Makes 10

50 g/2 oz pistachio nuts
125 g/4 oz self-raising flour
125 g/4 oz butter, softened
125 g/4 oz golden caster sugar
2 medium eggs, beaten
1 tbsp maple syrup or golden syrup

To decorate:

225 g/8 oz golden icing sugar
125 g/4 oz unsalted butter, softened
2 tsp lemon juice
25 g/1 oz pistachio nuts, chopped

Preheat the oven to 200°C/400°F/Gas Mark 6. Line a deep 12-hole muffin tray with 10 deep paper cases. Roughly chop the 50 g/2 oz pistachio nuts.

Sift the flour into a bowl and add the butter, sugar and eggs. Beat for about 2 minutes, then fold in the syrup and chopped nuts.

Spoon the mixture into the paper cases and bake for about 20 minutes until well risen and springy in the centre. Remove to a wire rack to cool.

To decorate the cakes, sift the icing sugar into a bowl, then add the butter, lemon juice and 1 tablespoon hot water. Beat until light and fluffy, then swirl onto each muffin with a small palette knife. Place the chopped pistachio nuts in a small shallow bowl. Dip the top of each muffin into the nuts to make an attractive topping. Keep for 4 days in an airtight container in a cool place.

Fondant Fancies

Makes 16–18

150 g/5 oz self-raising flour
150 g/5 oz caster sugar
50 g/2 oz ground almonds
150 g/5 oz butter, softened
3 medium eggs, beaten
4 tbsp milk

To decorate:

450 g/1 lb fondant icing sugar
paste food colourings
selection fancy cake decorations

Preheat the oven to 180°C/350°F/Gas Mark 4. Line two 12-hole bun trays with 16–18 paper cases, depending on the depth of the tray holes.

Sift the flour into a bowl and stir in the caster sugar and almonds. Add the butter, eggs and milk and beat until smooth.

Spoon into the paper cases and bake for 15–20 minutes until golden and firm to the touch. Turn out to cool on a wire rack. When cool, trim the tops flat if they have peaked slightly.

To decorate the cupcakes, make the fondant icing to a thick coating consistency, following the packet instructions. Divide into batches and colour each separately with a little paste food colouring. Keep each bowl covered with a damp cloth until needed. Spoon some icing over each cupcake, being sure to flood it right to the edge. Top each with a fancy decoration and leave to set for 30 minutes. Keep for 2 days in a cool place.

Crunchy-topped Citrus Chocolate Slices

Serves 12

175 g/6 oz butter
175 g/6 oz soft light brown sugar
finely grated zest of 1 orange
3 medium eggs, lightly beaten
1 tbsp ground almonds
175 g/6 oz self-raising flour
$^1/_4$ tsp baking powder
125 g/4 oz dark chocolate,
coarsely grated
2 tsp milk

For the crunchy topping:

125 g/4 oz granulated sugar
juice of 2 limes
juice of 1 orange

Preheat the oven to 170°C/325°F/Gas Mark 3, 10 minutes before baking. Oil and line a 28 x 18 x 2.5 cm/11 x 7 x 1 inch cake tin with nonstick baking parchment. Place the butter, sugar and orange zest into a large bowl and cream together until light and fluffy. Gradually add the eggs, beating after each addition, then beat in the ground almonds.

Sift the flour and baking powder into the creamed mixture. Add the grated chocolate and milk, then gently fold in using a metal spoon. Spoon the mixture into the prepared tin.

Bake on the centre shelf of the preheated oven for 35–40 minutes until well risen and firm to the touch. Leave in the tin for a few minutes to cool slightly. Turn out onto a wire rack and remove the baking parchment.

Meanwhile, to make the crunchy topping, place the sugar with the lime and orange juices into a small jug and stir together. Drizzle the sugar mixture over the hot cake, ensuring the whole surface is covered. Leave until completely cold, then cut into 12 slices and serve.

Magic Garden Cake

ℰ

Serves 20

For the cake base:

1 x 15 cm/6 inch, round lemon
Madeira cake (*see* page 29)
1 x 23 cm/9 inch, round lemon
Madeira cake
6 tbsp apricot glaze (*see* page)

To decorate:

15 cm/6 inch, round cake board
1.8 kg/4 lb ready-to-roll sugarpaste
blue, green, pink, yellow and purple
paste food colourings
icing sugar, for dusting
edible silver balls
black and green sugarcraft pens

Trim the tops of the cakes level if they have peaked, then brush the apricot glaze over the cakes. Colour 450 g/1 lb sugarpaste pale blue and use to cover the small cake. Trim the bottom neatly and lift the cake onto the cake card. Colour 900 g/2 lb sugarpaste pale green and use to cover the larger cake. Transfer this to a board or plate and put the smaller cake on top. Colour the trimmings of pale blue sugarpaste a deeper shade of blue. Roll into balls, about the size of a small pea, dampen these with cold boiled water and press them around the base of the smaller cake. Colour the trimmings of pale green sugarpaste a deeper shade of green.

Colour half the remaining sugarpaste deep pink and roll out a strip 1 cm/ ¹/₂ inch wide and long enough to go around the large cake. Mark lines along the edges of the strip, dampen and press around the base of the cake. Colour small pieces of the remaining sugarpaste pale pink, yellow and pale purple, leaving one piece white. Cut leaves and flower stalks from the green sugarpaste, then cut flowers from the pink or white sugarpaste and butterflies from the purple sugarpaste using butterfly cutters. Dampen the cut-outs and position as shown. Add flower centres using white or pink sugarpaste and details on the butterflies using yellow, pink and blue sugarpaste. Shape bees from yellow and white sugarpastes and press around the sides of the larger cake. Draw antennae on the butterflies (with edible silver balls on the tips) using a black sugarcraft pen and small trails of dots around the butterflies with a green pen, and mark lines on the wings with a knife. Add details to the flowers with the black pen and on the leaves with the green pen to finish.

Peaches & Cream Muffins

Makes 10

225 g/8 oz can peach slices
or halves in syrup
125 g/4 oz self-raising flour
50 g/2 oz wholemeal self-raising flour
$^1/_2$ tsp cinnamon
175 g/6 oz butter, softened
175 g/6 oz golden caster sugar
3 medium eggs, beaten
1 tbsp golden syrup

To decorate:

2 tsp lemon juice
2 tbsp icing sugar
150 ml/$^1/_4$ pint whipping cream

Preheat the oven to 190°C/375°F/Gas Mark 5. Line a deep 12-hole muffin tray with 10 paper cases. Drain the peaches and chop 125 g/4 oz into small chunks.

Sift the flours and cinnamon into a bowl, adding any bran from the sieve, then add the butter, sugar and eggs. Beat for about 2 minutes, then fold in the golden syrup and chopped peaches.

Spoon the mixture into the paper cases and bake for about 20 minutes until well risen and springy in the centre. Remove to a wire rack to cool.

Place 50 g/2 oz sliced peaches in a blender or food processor with the lemon juice and icing sugar to make a purée (the rest of the can's weight is syrup). Whip the cream until it forms soft peaks and then fold in half the purée. Place a large spoonful of cream on top of each muffin, then swirl in a little extra purée. Refrigerate until needed and eat within 24 hours.

Marbled Chocolate Traybake

Makes 8 Squares

175 g/6 oz butter
175 g/6 oz caster sugar
1 tsp vanilla extract
3 medium eggs, lightly beaten
200 g/7 oz self-raising flour
$1/2$ tsp baking powder
1 tbsp milk
$1^{1}/_2$ tbsp cocoa powder

For the chocolate icing:

75 g/3 oz dark chocolate,
broken into pieces
75 g/3 oz white chocolate,
broken into pieces

Preheat the oven to 180˚C/350˚F/Gas Mark 4, 10 minutes before baking. Oil and line a 28 x 18 x 2.5 cm/11 x 7 x 1 inch cake tin with nonstick baking parchment. Cream the butter, sugar and vanilla extract until light and fluffy. Gradually add the eggs, beating well after each addition. Sift in the flour and baking powder and fold in with the milk.

Spoon half the mixture into the prepared tin, spacing the spoonfuls apart and leaving gaps in between. Blend the cocoa powder to a smooth paste with 2 tablespoons warm water. Stir this into the remaining cake mixture. Drop small spoonfuls between the vanilla cake mixture to fill in all the gaps. Use a knife to swirl the mixtures together a little.

Bake on the centre shelf of the preheated oven for 35 minutes, or until well risen and firm to the touch. Leave in the tin for 5 minutes to cool, then turn out onto a wire rack and leave to cool. Remove the baking parchment.

For the icing, place the plain and white chocolate in separate heatproof bowls and melt each over a saucepan of almost boiling water. Spoon into separate nonstick baking parchment piping bags, snip off the tips and drizzle over the top. Leave to set before cutting into squares.

Pink Daisy Cake

Serves 12–14

For the cake base:

1 x 20 cm/8 inch round rich
fruit cake (*see* page 25),
covered in almond paste
(*see* page 45)

To decorate:

2 batches royal icing
(*see* page 41)
pink paste food colouring
125 g/4 oz ready-to-roll
sugarpaste icing
icing sugar, for dusting

Place the cake on a 25 cm/10 inch plate or cake board. Colour three quarters of the royal icing pale pink and spread half on top of the cake and work it over the surface with a paddling movement. Draw an icing ruler across the top of the cake at an angle and smooth back and forth until completely flat then leave the top to dry out for 4 hours.

Store the remaining royal icing in a plastic box with a tight-fitting lid or cover the bowl with a clean damp cloth. Ice the sides with the remaining pink icing. Remove any surplus icing and leave to dry out for 24 hours.

Roll out the sugarpaste thinly on a surface lightly dusted with icing sugar and stamp out 12 large daisies with a daisy cutter. Place the daisies on a sheet of nonstick baking parchment and pipe a small pink dot in the centre of each one. Leave to dry out for 24 hours.

Place the remaining white royal icing in a piping bag fitted with a medium plain nozzle. Pipe a border of small dots round the base of the cake then pipe dots over the top and sides. Dab the underside of each daisy with a little royal icing and stick round the top edge of the cake to form a border.

Light White Chocolate & Walnut Blondies

Serves 8

75 g/3 oz unsalted butter
200 g/7 oz demerara sugar
2 large eggs, lightly beaten
1 tsp vanilla extract
2 tbsp milk
125 g/4 oz plain flour, plus 1 tbsp
1 tsp baking powder
pinch salt
75 g/3 oz walnuts, roughly chopped
125 g/4 oz white chocolate drops
1 tbsp icing sugar, for dusting

Preheat the oven to 190°C/375°F/Gas Mark 5, 10 minutes before baking. Oil and line a 28 x 18 x 2.5 cm/11 x 7 x 1 inch cake tin with nonstick baking parchment. Place the butter and demerara sugar into a heavy-based saucepan and heat gently until the butter has melted and the sugar has started to dissolve. Remove from the heat and leave to cool.

Place the eggs, vanilla extract and milk in a large bowl and beat together. Stir in the butter and sugar mixture, then sift in the 125 g/4 oz of flour, the baking powder and salt. Gently stir the mixture twice.

Toss the walnuts and chocolate drops in the remaining 1 tablespoon of flour to coat. Add to the bowl and stir the ingredients together gently.

Spoon the mixture into the prepared tin and bake on the centre shelf of the preheated oven for 35 minutes, or until the top is firm and slightly crusty. Place the tin on a wire rack and leave to cool.

When completely cold, remove the cake from the tin and lightly dust the top with icing sugar. Cut into 16 blondies using a sharp knife, and serve.

Rhubarb ❧ Custard Muffins

Makes 12

225 g/8 oz pink rhubarb
25 g/1 oz vanilla custard powder
175 g/6 oz plain flour
2 tsp baking powder
125 g/4 oz golden caster sugar
100 ml/3^1/$_2$ fl oz milk
2 medium eggs, beaten
^{1}/$_2$ tsp vanilla extract
125 g/4 oz butter, melted and cooled
golden caster sugar, for dusting

Preheat the oven to 180°C/350°F/Gas Mark 4. Oil or line a 12-hole deep muffin tray with deep muffin cases. Chop the rhubarb into pieces 1 cm/^{1}/$_2$ inch long.

Sift the custard powder, flour and baking powder into a bowl and stir in the sugar. In another bowl, beat the milk, eggs and vanilla extract together. Make a well in the centre of the dry ingredients and pour in the milk mixture.

Add the melted butter and beat together with a fork until just combined, then fold in the chopped rhubarb. Spoon the mixture into the cases and bake for 15–20 minutes until golden, risen and firm in the centre.

Leave in the tray to firm up for 5 minutes, then turn out onto a wire rack to cool. Serve warm, dusted with golden caster sugar. Eat on the day of baking.

Ginger ❧ Apricot Mini Muffins

Makes 18

75 g/3 oz plain flour
75 g/3 oz wholemeal flour
2 tsp baking powder
$\frac{1}{2}$ tsp ground cinnamon
50 g/2 oz soft light brown sugar
1 medium egg
135 ml/$4\frac{1}{2}$ fl oz milk
75 g/3 oz butter, melted
125 g/4 oz canned apricots, drained
and finely chopped
50 g/2 oz glacé ginger, chopped
50 g/2 oz chopped almonds
sparkly sugar pieces, to decorate

Preheat the oven to 200°C/400°F/Gas Mark 6. Line one or two mini-muffin trays with 18 mini paper cases.

Sift the flours, baking powder and cinnamon into a bowl, adding any bran from the sieve, then stir in the sugar. In another bowl, beat the egg and milk together and then pour into the dry ingredients.

Add the melted butter, apricots, ginger and half the almonds and mix quickly with a fork until just combined.

Spoon the mixture into the cases. Scatter the other half of the almonds and the sugar crystals over the top. Bake for 15–20 minutes until risen and golden. Turn out onto a wire rack to cool and eat fresh on the day of baking.

Marmalade Loaf Cake

Serves 8–10

175 g/6 oz natural golden
caster sugar
175 g/6 oz butter, softened
3 medium eggs, beaten
175 g/6 oz self-raising flour
finely grated zest and juice
of 1 orange
100 g/3^1/$_2$ oz orange marmalade

For the topping:

zest and juice of 1 orange
125 g/4 oz icing sugar

Preheat the oven to 180°C/350°F/Gas Mark 4. Grease and line a
1 kg/2 lb loaf tin with a long thin strip of nonstick baking parchment.

Place the sugar and butter in a bowl and whisk until light and fluffy.
Add the beaten eggs a little at a time, adding 1 teaspoon flour with
each addition.

Add the remaining flour to the bowl with the orange zest, 2 tablespoons
orange juice and the marmalade. Using a large metal spoon, fold the
mixture together using a figure-of-eight movement until all the flour is
incorporated. Spoon the mixture into the tin and smooth level.

Bake for about 40 minutes until firm in the centre and a skewer inserted
into the centre comes out clean. Cool in the tin for 5 minutes, then turn
out to cool on a wire rack.

To make the topping, peel thin strips of zest away from the orange and
set aside. Squeeze the juice from the orange. Sift the icing sugar into a
bowl and mix with 1 tablespoon of the orange juice until a thin smooth
consistency forms. Drizzle over the top of the cake, letting it run down
the sides. Scatter over the orange zest and leave to set for 1 hour.

Apricot ❦ Almond Slice

Serves 10

2 tbsp demerara sugar
25 g/1 oz flaked almonds
400 g can apricot halves, drained
225 g/8 oz butter
225 g/8 oz caster sugar
4 medium eggs
200 g/7 oz self-raising flour
25 g/1 oz ground almonds
$^1/_2$ tsp almond extract
50 g/2 oz ready-to-eat dried
apricots, chopped
3 tbsp clear honey
3 tbsp roughly chopped
almonds, toasted

Preheat the oven to 180°C/350°F/Gas Mark 4. Oil a 20.5 cm/8 inch square tin and line with nonstick baking parchment.

Sprinkle the sugar and the flaked almonds over the paper, then arrange the apricot halves cut-side down on top.

Cream the butter and sugar together in a large bowl until light and fluffy.

Gradually beat the eggs into the butter mixture, adding a spoonful of flour after each addition of egg.

When all the eggs have been added, stir in the remaining flour and ground almonds and mix thoroughly.

Add the almond extract and the apricots and stir well.

Spoon the mixture into the prepared tin, taking care not to dislodge the apricot halves. Bake in the preheated oven for 1 hour, or until golden and firm to the touch.

Remove from the oven and allow to cool slightly for 15–20 minutes. Turn out carefully, discard the lining paper and transfer to a serving dish. Pour the honey over the top of the cake, sprinkle on the toasted almonds and serve.

Special Cakes for Every Day

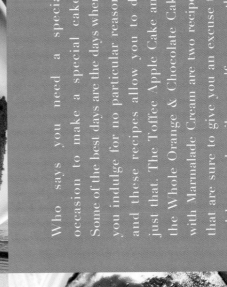
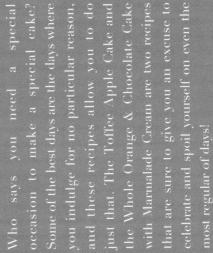

Who says you need a special occasion to make a special cake? Some of the best days are the days where you indulge for no particular reason, and these recipes allow you to do just that. The Toffee Apple Cake and the Whole Orange & Chocolate Cake with Marmalade Cream are two recipes that are sure to give you an excuse to celebrate and spoil yourself on even the most regular of days!

Lemon Bars

Makes 24

175 g/6 oz plain flour

125 g/4 oz butter

50 g/2 oz granulated sugar

200 g/7 oz caster sugar

2 tbsp plain flour

1/2 tsp baking powder

1/4 tsp salt

2 medium eggs,
lightly beaten

juice and finely grated
rind of 1 lemon

sifted icing sugar, to decorate

Preheat the oven to 170°C/325°F/Gas Mark 3, 10 minutes before baking. Lightly oil and line a 20.5 cm/8 inch square cake tin with greaseproof or baking paper.

Rub together the flour and butter until the mixture resembles breadcrumbs. Stir in the granulated sugar and mix.

Turn the mixture into the prepared tin and press down firmly. Bake in the preheated oven for 20 minutes, until pale golden.

Meanwhile, in a food processor, mix together the caster sugar, flour, baking powder, salt, eggs, lemon juice and rind until smooth. Pour over the prepared base.

Transfer to the preheated oven and bake for a further 20–25 minutes, until nearly set but still a bit wobbly in the centre. Remove from the oven and cool in the tin on a wire rack.

Dust with icing sugar and cut into squares. Serve cold or store in an airtight tin.

White Chocolate & Raspberry Mousse Gateau

Serves 8

125 g/4 oz caster sugar

75 g/3 oz plain flour, sifted

25 g/1 oz cornflour, sifted

3 gelatine leaves

450 g/1 lb raspberries,
thawed if frozen

400 g/14 oz white chocolate

200 g/7 oz plain fromage frais

2 medium egg whites

25 g/1 oz caster sugar

4 tbsp raspberry or orange liqueur

200 ml/7 fl oz double cream

fresh raspberries, halved,
to decorate

Preheat the oven to 190°C/375°F/Gas Mark 5, 10 minutes before baking. Oil and line two 23 cm/9 inch cake tins. Whisk the eggs and sugar until thick and creamy and the whisk leaves a trail in the mixture. Fold in the flour and cornflour, then divide between the tins. Bake in the oven for 12–15 minutes until risen and firm. Cool in the tins, then turn out onto wire racks.

Place the gelatine with 4 tablespoons cold water in a dish and leave to soften for 5 minutes. Purée half the raspberries, press through a sieve, then heat until nearly boiling. Squeeze out excess water from the gelatine, add to the purée and stir until dissolved. Reserve. Melt 175 g/6 oz of the chocolate in a bowl set over a saucepan of simmering water.

Leave to cool, then stir in the fromage frais and purée. Whisk the egg whites until stiff and whisk in the sugar. Fold into the raspberry mixture with the raspberries. Line the sides of a 23 cm/9 inch springform tin with baking parchment. Place 1 layer of cake in the base and sprinkle with half the liqueur. Pour in the raspberry mixture and top with the second cake. Brush with the remaining liqueur. Press down and chill for 4 hours.

Unmould onto a plate. Cut a strip of double thickness baking parchment to fit around and 1 cm/½ inch higher than the cake. Melt the remaining chocolate and spread thickly onto the parchment. Leave until just setting. Wrap around the cake and freeze for 15 minutes. Peel away the parchment. Whip the cream until thick and spread over the top. Decorate with raspberries.

Sachertorte

Serves 10-12

150 g/5 oz dark chocolate
150 g/5 oz unsalted butter, softened
125 g/4 oz caster sugar, plus 2 tbsp
3 medium eggs, separated
150 g/5 oz plain flour, sifted

To decorate:

225 g/8 oz apricot jam
125 g/4 oz dark chocolate, chopped
125 g/4 oz unsalted butter
25 g/1 oz milk chocolate

Preheat the oven to 180°C/350°F/Gas Mark 4, 10 minutes before baking. Lightly oil and line a deep, 23 cm/9 inch cake tin. Melt the 150 g/5 oz chocolate in a heatproof bowl over simmering water. Stir in 1 tablespoon water and leave to cool. Beat the butter and the 125 g/4 oz sugar together until light and fluffy. Beat in the egg yolks, one at a time, beating well after each addition. Stir in the melted chocolate, then the flour.

In a clean, grease-free bowl, whisk the egg whites until stiff peaks form, then whisk in the remaining sugar. Fold into the chocolate mixture and spoon into the prepared tin. Bake in the preheated oven for 30 minutes until firm. Leave for 5 minutes, then turn out onto a wire rack to cool. Leave the cake upside down. To decorate, split the cold cake in two. Heat the jam and sieve. Brush half the jam onto the first cake half, then cover with the remaining cake layer and brush with the remaining jam. Leave for 1 hour until the jam has set.

Melt the dark chocolate and the butter in a heatproof bowl over simmering water. Stir until smooth, then leave until thickened. Use to cover the cake. Melt the milk chocolate in a heatproof bowl over simmering water. With a small, greaseproof piping bag, pipe 'Sacher' with a large 'S' on the top. Leave to set.

Wild Strawberry & Rose Petal Jam Cake

Serves 8

275 g/10 oz plain flour

1 tsp baking powder

¼ tsp salt

150 g/5 oz unsalted butter, softened

200 g/7 oz caster sugar

2 large eggs, beaten

2 tbsp rosewater

125 ml/4 fl oz milk

125 g/4 oz rose petal or strawberry jam, slightly warmed

125 g/4 oz wild strawberries, hulled, or baby strawberries, chopped

frosted rose petals, to decorate

For the rose cream filling:

200 ml/7 fl oz double cream

25 ml/1 fl oz natural Greek yogurt

2 tbsp rosewater

1–2 tbsp icing sugar

Preheat the oven to 180°C/350°F/Gas Mark 4, 10 minutes before baking. Lightly oil and flour a 20.5 cm/8 inch nonstick cake tin. Sift the flour, baking powder and salt into a bowl and reserve.

Beat the butter and sugar until light and fluffy. Beat in the eggs, a little at a time, then stir in the rosewater. Gently fold in the flour mixture and milk with a metal spoon or rubber spatula and mix lightly together.

Spoon the cake mixture into the tin, spreading evenly and smoothing the top.

Bake in the preheated oven for 25–30 minutes until well risen and golden and the centre springs back when pressed with a clean finger. Remove and cool, then remove from the tin.

For the filling, whisk the cream, yogurt, 1 tablespoon of the rosewater and 1 tablespoon icing sugar until soft peaks form. Split the cake horizontally in half and sprinkle with the remaining rosewater.

Spread the warmed jam on the base of the cake. Top with half the whipped cream mixture, then sprinkle with half the strawberries. Place the remaining cake half on top. Spread with the remaining cream and swirl, if desired. Decorate with the rose petals. Dust the cake lightly with a little icing sugar and serve.

Indulgent Chocolate Squares

Serves 16

350 g/12 oz dark chocolate

175 g/6 oz butter, softened

175 g/6 oz soft light brown sugar

175 g/6 oz ground almonds

6 large eggs, separated

3 tbsp cocoa powder, sifted

75 g/3 oz fresh brown breadcrumbs

125 ml/4 fl oz double cream

50 g/2 oz white chocolate, chopped

50 g/2 oz milk chocolate, chopped

few freshly sliced strawberries,
to decorate

Preheat the oven to 180°C/350°F/Gas Mark 4, 10 minutes before baking. Oil and line a deep 20.5 cm/8 inch square cake tin with nonstick baking parchment. Melt 225 g/8 oz of the dark chocolate in a heatproof bowl set over a saucepan of almost boiling water. Stir until smooth, then leave until just cool, but not beginning to set.

Beat the butter and sugar until light and fluffy. Stir in the melted chocolate, ground almonds, egg yolks, cocoa powder and breadcrumbs. Whisk the egg whites until stiff peaks form, then stir a large spoonful into the chocolate mixture. Gently fold in the rest, then pour the mixture into the prepared tin.

Bake on the centre shelf in the preheated oven for 1¼ hours, or until firm, covering the top with foil after 45 minutes to prevent it over-browning. Leave in the tin for 20 minutes, then turn out onto a wire rack and leave to cool.

Melt the remaining 125 g/4 oz plain chocolate with the cream in a heatproof bowl set over a saucepan of almost boiling water, stirring occasionally. Leave to cool for 20 minutes, or until thickened slightly.

Spread the topping over the cake. Scatter over the white and milk chocolate and leave to set. Cut into 16 squares and serve decorated with a few freshly sliced strawberries, then serve.

Rich Chocolate Orange Mousse Dessert

Serves 8

225 g/8 oz plain dark chocolate, broken into pieces

8–12 sponge finger biscuits

225 g/8 oz unsalted butter

2 tbsp orange flower water

40 g/1½ oz cocoa powder, sifted

125 g/4 oz icing sugar, sifted

5 medium eggs, separated

50 g/2 oz caster sugar

1 orange, thinly sliced

300 ml/½ pint double cream

Oil and line a 900 g/2 lb loaf tin with clingfilm, taking care to keep the clingfilm as wrinkle free as possible. Arrange the sponge finger biscuits around the edge of the loaf tin, trimming the biscuits to fit if necessary.

Place the chocolate, butter and orange flower water in a heavy-based saucepan and heat gently, stirring occasionally, until the chocolate has melted and is smooth. Remove the saucepan from the heat, add the cocoa powder and 50 g/2 oz of the icing sugar. Stir until smooth, then beat in the egg yolks.

In a clean grease-free bowl whisk the egg whites until stiff but not dry. Sift in the remaining icing sugar and whisk until stiff and glossy. Fold the egg white mixture into the chocolate mixture and, using a metal spoon or rubber spatula, stir until well blended. Spoon the mousse mixture into the prepared loaf tin and level the surface. Cover and chill in the refrigerator until set.

Meanwhile, place the caster sugar with 150 ml/¼ pint of water in a heavy-based saucepan and heat until the sugar has dissolved. Bring to the boil and boil for 5 minutes. Add the orange slices and simmer for about 2–4 minutes or until the slices become opaque. Drain on absorbent kitchen paper, reserve. Trim the top of the biscuits to the same level as the mousse. Invert onto a plate and remove the tin and clingfilm.

Whip the cream until soft peaks form and spoon into a piping bag fitted with a star-shaped nozzle. Pipe swirls on top of the mousse and decorate with the orange slices. Chill in the refrigerator before serving.

Whole Orange & Chocolate Cake with Marmalade Cream

Serves 6-8

1 small orange, scrubbed
2 medium eggs, separated,
plus 1 whole egg
150 g/5 oz caster sugar
125 g/4 oz ground almonds
75 g/3 oz dark chocolate, melted
100 ml/3½ fl oz double cream
200 g/7 oz full-fat soft cheese
25 g/1 oz icing sugar
2 tbsp orange marmalade
orange zest, to decorate

Preheat the oven to 180°C/350°F/Gas Mark 4, 10 minutes before baking. Lightly oil and line the base of a 900 g/2 lb loaf tin. Place the orange in a small saucepan, cover with cold water and bring to the boil. Simmer for 1 hour until completely soft. Drain and leave to cool. Place 2 egg yolks, 1 whole egg and the sugar in a heatproof bowl set over a saucepan of simmering water and whisk until doubled in bulk. Remove from the heat and continue to whisk for 5 minutes until cooled.

Cut the whole orange in half and discard the seeds, then place into a food processor or blender and blend to a purée. Carefully fold the purée into the egg yolk mixture with the ground almonds and melted chocolate. Whisk the egg whites until stiff peaks form. Fold a large spoonful of the egg whites into the chocolate mixture, then gently fold the remaining egg whites into the mixture.

Pour into the tin and bake in the oven for 50 minutes, or until firm and a skewer inserted into the centre comes out clean. Cool in the tin before turning out and carefully discarding the lining paper. Meanwhile, whip the double cream until just thickened. In another bowl, blend the soft cheese with the icing sugar and marmalade until smooth, then fold in the double cream. Chill the marmalade cream in the refrigerator until required. Decorate with orange zest and serve the cake cut into slices with the marmalade cream.

Almond Angel Cake with Amaretto Cream

Serves 10–12

175 g/6 oz icing sugar,
plus 2–3 tbsp

150 g/5 oz plain flour

350 ml/12 fl oz egg whites
(about 10 large egg whites)

1½ tsp cream of tartar

½ tsp vanilla extract

1 tsp almond extract

¼ tsp salt

200 g/7 oz caster sugar

175 ml/6 fl oz double cream

2 tbsp amaretto liqueur

fresh raspberries, to decorate

Preheat the oven to 180°C/350°F/Gas Mark 4, 10 minutes before baking. Sift together the 175 g/6 oz icing sugar and flour. Stir to blend, then sift again and reserve. Using an electric whisk, beat the egg whites, cream of tartar, vanilla extract, ½ teaspoon of the almond extract and salt on medium speed until soft peaks form. Gradually add the caster sugar, 2 tablespoons at a time, beating well after each addition, until stiff peaks form.

Sift about one third of the flour mixture over the egg white mixture and gently fold in. Repeat, folding the flour mixture into the egg white mixture in two more batches. Spoon gently into an ungreased angel food cake tin or 25.5 cm/10 inch tube tin. Bake in the oven until risen and golden on top and the surface springs back quickly when gently pressed with a clean finger. Immediately invert the cake tin and cool completely in the tin.

When cool, carefully run a sharp knife around the edge of the tin and the centre ring to loosen the cake from the edge. Using the fingertips, ease the cake from the tin and invert onto a cake plate. Thickly dust the cake with the extra icing sugar. Whip the cream with the remaining almond extract, liqueur and a little more icing sugar until soft peaks form. Fill a piping bag fitted with a star nozzle with half the cream and pipe around the bottom edge of the cake. Decorate the edge with the fresh raspberries and serve the remaining cream separately.

Chocolate Bonbons Cake

Serves 24

For the cake base:

1 x 25 cm/10 inch round
chocolate cake (see page 28)

To decorate:

2 tbsp orange liqueur or
orange juice

1 batch vanilla buttercream

900 g/2 lb ready-to-roll sugarpaste

cream and light brown paste
food colourings

icing sugar, for dusting

125 g/4 oz white chocolate, melted

30 dark chocolate truffles

125 g/4 oz toasted chopped
hazlenuts

Trim the top of the cake flat if it has peaked. Beat the orange liqueur or juice into the buttercream. Cut the cake in half horizontally and spread with a little buttercream, then replace the top and spread buttercream over the top and sides of the cake.

Colour three quarters of the sugarpaste pale cream with a little paste food colouring, then roll out the sugarpaste on a surface lightly dusted with icing sugar to a circle large enough to cover the cake. Carefully lift this over the cake, then smooth down and trim away the edges.

Colour the scraps and remaining sugarpaste light brown. Roll out thinly on a surface lightly dusted with icing sugar and, using a pasta wheel, cut out thin strips 1 cm/½ inch wide. Brush the underside of the fluted strips with a little cold boiled water and stick around the sides of the cake at regular intervals. Trim the tops of the strips level with a sharp knife.

Place the melted white chocolate in a small paper icing bag. Snip a small hole at the top and pipe whirls round 10 of the truffles. Spread a little of the remaining melted chocolate over 10 more truffles and roll them in chopped hazelnuts. Place the chocolates alternately in plain, chopped nuts and whirl patterns around the base of the cake. Arrange 9 truffles on top of the cake as shown.

Lemon-iced Ginger Squares

Makes 12

225 g/8 oz caster sugar
50 g/2 oz butter, melted
2 tbsp black treacle
2 medium egg whites,
lightly whisked
225 g/8 oz plain flour
1 tsp bicarbonate of soda
½ tsp ground cloves
1 tsp ground cinnamon
¼ tsp ground ginger
pinch salt
225 ml/8 fl oz buttermilk
175 g/6 oz icing sugar
2–4 tbsp lemon juice

Preheat the oven to 200°C/400°F/Gas Mark 6, 15 minutes before baking. Lightly oil a 20.5 cm/8 inch square cake tin and sprinkle with a little flour.

Mix together the caster sugar, butter and treacle. Stir in the egg whites.

In a separate bowl, mix together the flour, bicarbonate of soda, cloves, cinnamon, ginger and salt. Stir the flour mixture and buttermilk alternately into the butter mixture until blended well.

Spoon into the prepared tin and bake in the preheated oven for 35 minutes, or until a skewer inserted into the centre of the cake comes out clean.

Remove from the oven and allow to cool for 5 minutes in the tin before turning out on to a wire rack over a large plate. Using a cocktail stick, make holes on the top of the cake.

Meanwhile, mix together the icing sugar with enough lemon juice to make a smooth pourable icing. Carefully pour the icing over the hot cake, then leave until cold. Cut the ginger cake into squares and serve.

Toffee Apple Cake

Serves 8

2 small eating apples, peeled

4 tbsp soft dark brown sugar

175 g/6 oz butter or margarine

175 g/6 oz caster sugar

3 medium eggs

175 g/6 oz self-raising flour

150 ml/¹/₄ pint double cream

2 tbsp icing sugar

¹/₂ tsp vanilla extract

¹/₂ tsp ground cinnamon

Preheat the oven to 180°C/350°F/Gas Mark 4, 10 minutes before baking. Lightly oil and line the bases of 2 x 20.5 cm/8 inch sandwich tins with greaseproof or baking paper.

Thinly slice the apples and toss in the brown sugar until well coated. Arrange them over the bases of the prepared tins and reserve.

Cream together the butter or margarine and caster sugar until light and fluffy. Beat the eggs together in a small bowl and gradually beat them into the creamed mixture, beating well after each addition.

Sift the flour into the mixture and, using a metal spoon or rubber spatula, fold in. Divide the mixture between the two cake tins and level the surface.

Bake in the preheated oven for 25–30 minutes until golden and well risen. Leave in the tins to cool.

Lightly whip the cream with 1 tablespoon of the icing sugar and the vanilla extract. Sandwich the cakes together with the cream. Mix the remaining icing sugar and the ground cinnamon together, sprinkle over the top of the cake and serve.

Dundee Cake

Serves 8-10

400 g/14 oz mixed dried fruit

50 g/2 oz ground almonds

finely grated zest and juice
of 1 lemon

150 g/5 oz butter, at
room temperature

150 g/5 oz natural golden
caster sugar

3 medium eggs, beaten

125 g/4 oz plain flour

40 g/1½ oz whole blanched
almonds

Preheat the oven to 180°C/350°F/Gas Mark 4. Grease and line the base of an 18 cm/7 inch deep round cake tin with nonstick baking parchment.

Place the dried fruit in a bowl and stir in the ground almonds to coat the dried fruit.

Finely grate the zest from the lemon into the bowl, then squeeze out 1 tablespoon of juice and add to the same bowl. In another bowl, beat the butter and sugar together until light and fluffy. Whisk in the eggs a little at a time, adding 1 teaspoon of the flour with each addition.

Sift in the remaining flour, then add the fruit and almond mixture. Fold together with a large metal spoon until smooth. Spoon the mixture into the tin and make a dip in the centre with the back of a spoon. Arrange the almonds over the top in circles.

Bake for 1 hour, then reduce the heat to 150°C/300°F/Gas Mark 2 and bake for a further hour, or until a skewer inserted into the centre comes out clean. Cool in the tin for 5 minutes, then turn out to cool on a wire rack.

Apple & Cinnamon Crumble Bars

Makes 16

450 g/1 lb Bramley cooking apples,
roughly chopped

50 g/2 oz raisins

50 g/2 oz caster sugar

1 tsp ground cinnamon

zest of 1 lemon

200 g/7 oz plain flour

250 g/9 oz soft light brown sugar

1/2 tsp bicarbonate of soda

150 g/5 oz rolled oats

150 g/5 oz butter, melted

crème fraîche or whipped cream,
to serve

Preheat the oven to 190°C/375°F/Gas Mark 5, 10 minutes before baking. Place the apples, raisins, sugar, cinnamon and lemon zest into a saucepan over a low heat.

Cover and cook for about 15 minutes, stirring occasionally, until the apple is cooked through. Remove the cover, stir well to break up the apple completely with a wooden spoon.

Cook for a further 15–30 minutes over a very low heat until reduced, thickened and slightly darkened. Allow to cool. Lightly oil and line a 20.5 cm/8 inch square cake tin with greaseproof or baking paper.

Mix together the flour, sugar, bicarbonate of soda, rolled oats and butter until combined well and crumbly.

Spread half of the flour mixture into the bottom of the prepared tin and press down. Pour over the apple mixture.

Sprinkle over the remaining flour mixture and press down lightly. Bake in the preheated oven for 30–35 minutes, until golden brown.

Remove from the oven and allow to cool before cutting into slices. Serve the bars warm or cold with crème fraîche or whipped cream.

Almond Cake

Serves 8

225 g/8 oz butter or margarine
225 g/8 oz caster sugar
3 large eggs
1 tsp vanilla extract
1 tsp almond extract
125 g/4 oz self-raising flour
175 g/6 oz ground almonds
50 g/2 oz whole,
blanched almonds
25 g/1 oz plain dark chocolate

Preheat the oven to 150°C/300°F/Gas Mark 2. Lightly oil and line the base of a 20.5 cm/8 inch, deep, round cake tin with greaseproof or baking paper.

Cream together the butter or margarine and sugar with a wooden spoon until light and fluffy. Beat the eggs and extract together. Gradually add to the sugar and butter mixture and mix well after each addition.

Sift the flour and mix with the ground almonds. Beat into the egg mixture until well mixed and smooth. Pour into the prepared cake tin. Roughly chop the whole almonds and scatter over the cake.

Bake in the preheated oven for 45 minutes, or until golden and risen and a skewer inserted into the centre of the cake comes out clean. Remove from the tin and leave to cool on a wire rack.

Melt the chocolate in a small bowl placed over a saucepan of gently simmering water, stirring until smooth and free of lumps. Drizzle the melted chocolate over the cooled cake and serve once the chocolate has set.

Blueberry Buttermilk Muffins

Makes 6–8

175 g/6 oz plain flour
1 tsp baking powder
175 g/6 oz golden caster sugar
175 ml/6 fl oz buttermilk
1 medium egg
½ tsp vanilla extract
40 g/1½ oz butter, melted
and cooled
150 g/5 oz fresh blueberries

Preheat the oven to 180°C/350°F/Gas Mark 4. Line a deep muffin tray with 6–8 paper cases, depending on the depth of the holes.

Sift the flour and baking powder into a bowl, then add the sugar. In another bowl, beat the buttermilk with the egg and vanilla extract, then pour into the dry ingredients. Mix with a fork, then add the cooled melted butter and stir until mixed but still slightly lumpy.

Gently fold in the blueberries. Spoon the mixture into the muffin cases, filling each two-thirds full. Bake for about 20 minutes until springy in the centre. Leave in the trays for 5 minutes, then turn out onto a wire rack to finish cooling. Eat warm or cold on the day of baking.

Fresh Strawberry Sponge Cake

Serves 8–10

175 g/6 oz unsalted butter, softened

175 g/6 oz caster sugar

1 tsp vanilla extract

3 large eggs, beaten

175 g/6 oz self-raising flour

150 ml/¼ pint double cream

2 tbsp icing sugar, sifted

225 g/8 oz fresh strawberries, hulled and chopped

few extra strawberries, to decorate

Preheat the oven to 190°C/375°F/Gas Mark 5, 10 minutes before baking. Lightly oil and line the bases of two 20.5 cm/ 8 inch round cake tins with greaseproof paper or baking parchment.

Using an electric whisk, beat the butter, sugar and vanilla extract until pale and fluffy. Gradually beat in the eggs a little at a time, beating well after each addition.

Sift half the flour over the mixture and, using a metal spoon or rubber spatula, gently fold into the mixture. Sift over the remaining flour and fold in until just blended.

Divide the mixture between the tins, spreading evenly. Gently smooth the surfaces with the back of a spoon. Bake in the centre of the preheated oven for 20–25 minutes until well risen and golden.

Remove and leave to cool before turning out onto a wire rack. Whip the cream with 1 tablespoon of the icing sugar until it forms soft peaks. Fold in the chopped strawberries.

Spread one cake layer evenly with the mixture and top with the second cake layer, rounded-side up. Thickly dust the cake with icing sugar and decorate with the reserved strawberries. Carefully slide onto a serving plate and serve.

Fat-free Sponge

Serves 8

175 g/6 oz caster sugar, plus extra
for dusting

3 medium eggs

125 g/4 oz self-raising flour, plus
extra for dusting

To decorate:

150 ml/1/4 pint low-fat whipping
cream, or low-fat crème fraîche
or yogurt

2 tbsp lemon curd

125 g/4 oz blueberries

zest of 1 lemon, cut into long
thin strips

Preheat the oven to 190°C/375°F/Gas Mark 5. Grease two nonstick 18 cm/7 inch sandwich tins, line with nonstick baking parchment, then dust with a mixture of flour and caster sugar.

Put the eggs and sugar in a large bowl and stand this over a pan of simmering water. Whisk the eggs and sugar until doubled in volume and the mixture is thick enough to leave a trail on the surface of the batter when the whisk is lifted away.

Remove the bowl from the heat and continue whisking for a further 5 minutes until the mixture is cool. Sift half the flour over the mixture and fold in very lightly, using a large metal spoon. Sift in the remaining flour and fold in the same way.

Pour the mixture into the tins and tilt them to spread the mixture evenly. Bake for 15–20 minutes until well risen and firm and the cakes are beginning to shrink away from the sides of the tins. Leave to stand for 2 minutes, then turn out to cool on a wire rack.

To decorate, whip the cream, if using, and spread half the cream (or crème fraîche or yogurt) over one cake. Swirl 1 tablespoon of the lemon curd into the cream, crème fraîche or yogurt and scatter over half the blueberries. Place the other cake on top and swirl over the remaining cream/yogurt. Swirl over the remaining lemon curd and sprinkle with the remaining berries. Scatter the strips of lemon zest over the top.

Coffee & Walnut Muffins

Makes 12

125 g/4 oz butter, softened

125 g/4 oz soft light brown sugar

150 g/5 oz plain flour

1 tsp baking powder

2 medium eggs

1 tbsp golden syrup

1 tsp vanilla extract

4 tbsp sour cream

40 g/1½ oz walnut pieces,
chopped

To decorate:

150 ml/¼ pint double cream

1 tbsp golden caster sugar

1 tsp coffee extract

½ tsp ground cinnamon

50 g/2 oz walnut pieces

Preheat the oven to 180°C/350°F/Gas Mark 4. Grease or line a 12-hole muffin tray with paper cases.

Beat the butter and sugar together until light and fluffy. Sift in the flour and baking powder, then add the eggs, golden syrup, vanilla extract and soured cream. Beat together until fluffy, then fold in the nuts.

Spoon the batter into the paper cases, filling them about three-quarters full. Bake for about 25 minutes until a skewer inserted into the centre comes out clean. Turn out to cool on a wire rack.

For the topping, put the cream, sugar, coffee extract and cinnamon in a bowl and whisk until soft peaks form. Swirl over the muffins and top each with a walnut piece. Refrigerate until needed, or keep chilled for 24 hours in an airtight container.

Supreme Chocolate Gateau

Serves 10-12

For the cake:

175 g/6 oz self-raising
flour, sifted

1½ tsp baking powder, sifted

3 tbsp cocoa powder, sifted

175 g/6 oz margarine or
butter, softened

175 g/6 oz caster sugar

3 large eggs

To decorate:

350 g/12 oz dark chocolate

1 gelatine leaf

200 ml/7 fl oz double cream

75 g/3 oz butter

cocoa powder, for dusting

Preheat the oven to 180°C/350°F/Gas Mark 4. Line three 20.5 cm/8 inch, round tins. Put all the cake ingredients in a bowl and whisk. Divide between the tins, then bake in the oven for 35–40 minutes. Cool on wire racks. Heat 2 tablespoons hot water with 50 g/2 oz of the chocolate and combine. Take off the heat and leave for 5 minutes.

Put the gelatine in a shallow dish and add 2 tablespoons cold water. Leave for 5 minutes, then squeeze out any excess water and add to the chocolate and water mixture. Stir until dissolved. Whip the double cream until just thickened. Add the chocolate mixture and continue whisking. Leave until starting to set. Place one of the cakes onto a plate and spread with half the cream mixture. Top with a second cake and the remaining cream. Cover with the third cake and refrigerate until set.

Melt half the chocolate with the butter, stir until smooth and leave until thickened. Melt the remaining chocolate. Cut 12 10 cm/4 inch squares of foil. Spread the chocolate over the squares to within 2.5 cm/1 inch of the edges. Refrigerate for 3–4 minutes; gather up the corners and crimp. Refrigerate until firm. Spread the chocolate and butter mixture over the top and sides of the cake. Remove the foil from the curls and use to decorate. Dust with cocoa powder and serve.

Very Berry Muffins

Makes 10

225 g/8 oz plain flour

1 tsp baking powder

1/2 tsp bicarbonate of soda

65 g/2½ oz golden caster sugar

1 medium egg

175 ml/6 fl oz milk

zest and 1 tbsp juice from

1 small orange

50 g/2 oz butter, melted and cooled

125 g/4 oz fresh raspberries

50 g/2 oz dried cranberries

Preheat the oven to 200°C/400°F/Gas Mark 6. Line a deep 12-hole muffin tray with 10 deep paper cases.

Sift the flour, baking powder and bicarbonate of soda into a large bowl. Add the sugar and make a well in the centre. Beat the egg and milk together in a jug with the orange juice.

Pour the milk mixture into the bowl together with the cooled butter and the orange zest and beat lightly with a fork until all the flour is combined but the mixture is still slightly lumpy. Gently fold in the raspberries and cranberries and spoon into the paper cases.

Bake for about 20 minutes until firm and risen and a skewer inserted into the centre comes out clean. Cool on a wire rack. Eat warm or cold on the day of baking.

Chocolate Fudge Brownies

Makes 16

125 g/4 oz butter

175 g/6 oz plain dark chocolate,
roughly chopped or broken

225 g/8 oz caster sugar

2 tsp vanilla extract

2 medium eggs, lightly beaten

150 g/5 oz plain flour

175 g/6 oz icing sugar

2 tbsp cocoa powder

15 g/½ oz butter

Preheat the oven to 180°C/350°F/Gas Mark 4, 10 minutes before baking. Lightly oil and line a 20.5 cm/8 inch square cake tin with greaseproof or baking paper.

Slowly melt the butter and chocolate together in a heatproof bowl set over a sauce-pan of simmering water. Transfer the mixture to a large bowl.

Stir in the sugar and vanilla extract, then stir in the eggs. Sift over the flour and fold together well with a metal spoon or rubber spatula. Pour into the prepared tin.

Transfer to the preheated oven and bake for 30 minutes until just set. Remove the cooked mixture from the oven and leave to cool in the tin before turning it out on to a wire rack.

Sift the icing sugar and cocoa powder into a small bowl and make a well in the centre.

Place the butter in the well then gradually add about 2 tablespoons of hot water. Mix to form a smooth spreadable icing.

Pour the icing over the cooked mixture. Allow the icing to set before cutting into squares. Serve the brownies when they are cold.

Chocolate Nut Brownies

Makes 16

125 g/4 oz butter

150 g/5 oz soft light brown sugar

50 g/2 oz plain dark chocolate,
roughly chopped or broken

2 tbsp smooth peanut butter

2 medium eggs

50 g/2 oz unsalted roasted peanuts,
finely chopped

100 g/3½ oz self-raising flour

For the topping:

125 g/4 oz plain dark chocolate,
roughly chopped or broken

50 ml/2 fl oz soured cream

Preheat the oven to 180°C/350°F/Gas Mark 4, 10 minutes before baking. Lightly oil and line a 20.5 cm/8 inch square cake tin with greaseproof or baking paper.

Combine the butter, sugar and chocolate in a small saucepan and heat gently until the sugar and chocolate have melted, stirring constantly. Reserve and cool slightly.

Mix together the peanut butter, eggs and peanuts in a large bowl.

Stir in the cooled chocolate mixture. Sift in the flour and fold together with a metal spoon or rubber spatula until combined.

Pour into the prepared tin and bake in the preheated oven for about 30 minutes, or until just firm.

Cool for 5 minutes in the tin before turning out on to a wire rack to cool.

To make the topping, melt the chocolate in a heatproof bowl over a saucepan of simmering water, making sure that the base of the bowl does not touch the water.

Cool slightly, then stir in the soured cream until smooth and glossy. Spread over the brownies, refrigerate until set, then cut into squares. Serve the brownies cold.

Chocolate ❧ Coconut Cake

Serves 8

125 g/4 oz dark chocolate,
roughly chopped

175 g/6 oz butter or margarine

175 g/6 oz caster sugar

3 medium eggs, beaten

175 g/6 oz self-raising flour

1 tbsp cocoa powder

50 g/2 oz desiccated coconut

For the icing:

125 g/4 oz butter or margarine

2 tbsp creamed coconut

225 g/8 oz icing sugar

25 g/1 oz desiccated coconut,
lightly toasted

Preheat the oven to 180°C/350°F/Gas Mark 4, 10 minutes before baking. Melt the chocolate in a small bowl over a saucepan of gently simmering water, ensuring that the base of the bowl does not touch the water. When the chocolate has melted, stir until smooth and let cool.

Lightly oil and line the bases of two 18 cm/7 inch sandwich tins with greaseproof paper. In a large bowl, beat the butter or margarine and sugar together with a wooden spoon until light and creamy. Beat in the eggs a little at a time, then stir in the melted chocolate. Sift the flour and cocoa powder together and gently fold into the chocolate mixture. Add the desiccated coconut and mix lightly. Divide between the two tins and smooth the tops. Bake in the preheated oven for 25–30 minutes until a skewer comes out clean when inserted into the centre of the cake. Allow to cool in the tins for 5 minutes, then turn out, discard the lining paper and leave on a wire rack until cold.

Beat together the butter or margarine and creamed coconut until light. Add the icing sugar and mix well. Spread half of the icing on one cake and press the cakes together. Spread the remaining icing over the top, sprinkle with the coconut and serve.

Victoria Sponge with Mango & Mascarpone

Serves 8

175 g/6 oz caster sugar,
plus extra for dusting

175 g/6 oz self-raising flour,
plus extra for dusting

175 g/6 oz butter or margarine

3 large eggs

1 tsp vanilla extract

25 g/1 oz icing sugar

250 g/9 oz mascarpone cheese

1 large ripe mango, peeled

Preheat the oven to 190°C/375°F/Gas Mark 5, 10 minutes before baking. Lightly oil two 18 cm/7 inch sandwich tins and lightly dust with caster sugar and flour, tapping the tins to remove any excess.

In a large bowl, cream the butter or margarine and sugar together with a wooden spoon until light and creamy. In another bowl, mix the eggs and vanilla extract together. Sift the flour several times onto a plate. Beat a little egg into the butter and sugar, then a little flour and beat well.

Continue adding the flour and eggs alternately, beating after each addition, until the mixture is well mixed and smooth. Divide between the two cake tins, level the surface, then, using the back of a large spoon, make a slight dip in the centre of each cake.

Bake in the oven for 25–30 minutes until the centre of the cake springs back when gently pressed with a clean finger. Turn out onto a wire rack and leave the cakes until cold.

Beat the icing sugar and mascarpone cheese together, then chop the mango into small cubes. Use half the mascarpone and mango to sandwich the cakes together. Spread the rest of the mascarpone on top, decorate with the remaining mango and serve. Otherwise, lightly cover and store in the refrigerator.

All-in-one Chocolate Fudge Cakes

Makes 15 squares

175 g/6 oz soft dark brown sugar

175 g/6 oz butter, softened
150 g/5 oz self-raising flour
25 g/1 oz cocoa powder
1/2 tsp baking powder
pinch salt
3 medium eggs, lightly beaten
1 tbsp golden syrup

For the fudge topping:

75 g/3 oz granulated sugar
150 ml/1/4 pint evaporated milk
175 g/6 oz plain dark chocolate,
roughly chopped
40 g/1 1/2 oz unsalted butter, softened
125 g/4 oz soft fudge sweets,
finely chopped

Preheat the oven to 180°C/350°F/Gas Mark 4, 10 minutes before baking. Oil and line a 28 x 18 x 2.5 cm/11 x 7 x 1 inch cake tin with nonstick baking parchment.

Place the soft brown sugar and butter in a bowl and sift in the flour, cocoa powder, baking powder and salt. Add the eggs and golden syrup, then beat with an electric whisk for 2 minutes, before adding 2 tablespoons warm water and beating for a further 1 minute.

Turn the mixture into the prepared tin and level the top with the back of a spoon. Bake on the centre shelf of the preheated oven for 30 minutes, or until firm to the touch. Turn the cake out onto a wire rack and leave to cool before removing the baking parchment.

To make the topping, gently heat the sugar and evaporated milk in a saucepan, stirring frequently, until the sugar has dissolved. Bring the mixture to the boil and simmer for 6 minutes, without stirring.

Remove the mixture from the heat. Add the chocolate and butter and stir until melted and blended. Pour into a bowl and chill in the refrigerator for 1–2 hours until thickened. Spread the topping over the cake, then sprinkle with the chopped fudge. Cut the cake into 15 squares before serving.

Index

Special Cakes